YOUR
Freaking Amazing
GIFTS

A STEP-BY-STEP GUIDE TO DEVELOP YOUR INTUITION AND MEDIUMSHIP MUSCLES

BY BRANDALEEN JOHNSON

COPYRIGHT

Copyright@ 2016 Brandaleen Johnson.

All rights reserved.

Brandaleen Johnson 8801 E. Angus Road, Traverse City, MI 49684

For information about special discounts available for bulk purchases, sales promotions, fund-raising, and educational needs, contact Brandaleen Johnson at 231-313-1601 or at brandaleen@yahoo.com

Find out more about the author at www.brandaleen.com.

First Edition.

ISBN-13: 978-1537380247

ISBN-10: 1537380249

Cover & Design by: Sky Wonders
Editor: Sophia Collins

TABLE OF CONTENTS

COPYRIGHT 3
TABLE OF CONTENTS 4
DEDICATION 6
PREFACE 7
INTRODUCTION 8
CHAPTER 1: WHY CONNECT TO YOUR INTUITION 13
CHAPTER 2: INTENTION 18
CHAPTER 3: JOURNALING 22
CHAPTER 4: MEDITATION 25
CHAPTER 5: RAISE YOUR VIBRATION. 30
CHAPTER 6: PINEAL GLAND, THE SEAT TO YOUR SOUL 37
CHAPTER 7: SELF-CARE 41
CHAPTER 8: PROTECTION 45
CHAPTER 9: AGREEMENTS 53
CHAPTER 10: MEET YOUR SPIRIT GUIDES 57
CHAPTER 11: ANGELS 64
CHAPTER 12 ETHICS AND NON-JUDGEMENT 72
CHAPTER 13: HOW TO APPROACH GAMES AND READINGS 76
CHAPTER 14: CLAIRVOYANCE 80
CHAPTER 15: CLAIRAUDIENCE 85

CHAPTER 16: CLAIRSENTIENCE 91
CHAPTER 17: CLAIRCOGNIZANCE 95
CHAPTER 18: EMPATHY 97
CHAPTER 19: MEDIUMSHIP 101
CHAPTER 20: IN CLOSING 111

Dedication

During a deep meditation in January 2014, Archangel Gabriel came to me and handed me a giant pen. After meditation, I wrote in my journal, "I think he wants me to write a book." Well, here it is, and I couldn't have done it without Gabriel, the Angels, my guides, and pure consciousness itself. Therefore, I dedicate this book to Source, God, The Universe, and All That Is.

Preface

From being considered a "normal" member of society to being able to speak to the dead, Brandaleen shares her step-by-step process on how she developed her intuition and mediumship. She shares with readers her passion about connecting to what we came equipped with in order to create our best human experience. Her high vibes and spunky energy shines through in this easy conversational read. Brandaleen's journey is enlightening and includes a road map that anyone can apply to safely develop their very own special gifts.

It is recommended that this book be read at a pace that allows you to do the exercises in each chapter to ensure the reader has the intended experience and results.

You can find out more about Brandaleen and connect with her by visiting her website at brandaleen.com

Introduction

I am so excited that the Universe guided you to this book! There're no coincidences in my world!

So check this out! We are about to go on a little journey together. A journey of re-awakening, self-discovery, and developing what lies inside you! That's intimate so before we get started I want to share how I became to be the person writing this book!

Today I have many titles such as psychic medium, author, business coach, educator, and speaker but what it all comes down to is I help people like you create the life they want through spiritual and personal development. The part of my story that surprises most people is I wasn't always psychic. You see, once upon a time, I lived in Las Vegas, Nevada and I was living life just like you. I had various jobs growing up and eventually settled in and worked over 15 years in commercial real estate as a marketing specialist. I was working, not because I loved it, but because that was what I was supposed to do as a member of society. I was the perfect member of society. I had lots of things and lots of debt, and I was not anywhere near happy.

Sure, I have been a bit mystical since a young age. I loved receiving tarot readings when I'd go to Renaissance fairs or the like. My mother influenced me as well because she liked to go to seminars with speakers talking about spiritual things such as Angelic Healers, past life experiences and near death experiences, and even people who would talk about remote viewing, astral projection, and UFOs. This was always fascinating to me.

It was during my first marriage that I was at one of those seminars with my mom and the lady sitting next to me started talking about Reiki, a hands-on healing modality that transfers Source energy through the practitioner and into their client. I thought, "How freaking cool is this?" All I had to do was find a Reiki master, take a class and TA DAH, become a healer? Sign me up!

Shortly after, I had found a Reiki Master, who agreed to teach me, located in San Diego, California. My best friend just so happened to live in Newport Beach so off I went for a long weekend of HOLY ENERGY transformation, Batman!

The night I received my first Reiki attunement, where the gift of Reiki is passed down to you, I was on my way back to my friend's house and suddenly the entire car filled with the aroma of pizza. A few minutes later I arrived at my friend's house to see pizza had just been delivered. I was so blown away by this! That, my friends, was my first intuitive experience that I can consciously recall.

After that, I had dabbled in learning about crystals, reflexology, and other things that fall under this category, but as for the Reiki, I, like many, was fearful to start a practice or do it professionally. At that time it was new, and no one had heard of it, not to mention I let fear block me in moving forward with that. For the next 14 years, I left all of this behind and focused on raising my daughter, working and paying bills. Until one day my second husband, my daughter, and I went on a vacation to Traverse City, MI. There was something about the energy of the Grand Traverse Bay that captivated me like nothing ever had. Six weeks later we lived here, but that's all part of another story I tell in my book, Your Freaking Amazing Life!

What happened after we moved to Michigan was nothing less than a miracle. It seems that everything happened at once and for me to pinpoint one thing that really catapulted me to being the psychic medium that I am is difficult. I, however, want to share what I believe were the most important factors to my growth.

Reiki

I started to do Reiki professionally in Traverse City alongside an online nutrition company that I founded and operated, and that's when I began to sense things during these Reiki sessions. I would start to see images and feelings about my client's life in my head during sessions. At first, I thought it was my imagination until I started to share with my clients. They would give me validation and tell me what I saw and felt was actually true. One example was I saw my client on a boat in a long white dress, and she confirmed she had just gone on a cruise. Simple things like this intrigued me. How cool, right?

Nature

Moving from living 27 years in the desert in Las Vegas, NV to a rural country town in the midst of the most stunning nature, in Traverse City, MI has played a huge role in my awakening. I knew it from the moment I "felt" the energy of the bay before we even lived here. I would walk into the forest of hardwoods near my house, and I could sense the air would almost stop moving and feel like I had eyes watching me. I would sit with my back to a tree and look up and see invisible balls of energy moving. When I say invisible, it is almost like how we see gas fumes. These balls would move around the leaves, and I came to know them as tree fairies. You should try it and see if you can see them.

A Slower Life

The change from living in the city to living in the country was also reality changing for me. It wasn't just the slower life, but I believe the air quality and water quality were essential for my vibration to raise.

I Exercised My Muscles! (The most important part ever!)

During all of this, I saw an online course offered by a medium talking about meeting your spirit guides. Hey, that was right up my alley! So I signed right up! Once I got over thinking I was crazy or making it up about my spirit guides, that's when I realized there is WAY more to life than just paying bills and dying. Just that one simple thing was like an AH HA moment for my entire belief system. But it didn't stop there. I ended up developing all of my intuitive muscles and fast.

It was after all of this that I said to myself, "This can't stop with me. I have to help people stuck in their daily human lives understand the following: we are not here to just pay bills and die; we all have these special gifts; we all have a special job to do; understanding and awakening to our gifts can change the world."

It was through my journey that I came to understand the "we are one" concept. I came to understand my ego and how I was letting it run my life. I came to understand my personal power and that each one of us has it.

That's when I looked at every step I took to get here and developed my online courses to help others do the same. Since then, I have witnessed the transformation of so many of students' lives.

Can you imagine having my job and seeing someone go from zero to holding gallery readings? (Gallery readings are done in a group setting or stadium setting when the medium can receive messages from several spirits in one session.) How about channeling angels, becoming an intuitive life coach, medical intuitive, or even more in touch with your higher self to help you make the best decisions in your life? I just love my job!

Now that we had a little bonding time let's get to the good stuff!

Chapter 1: Why Connect To Your Intuition

*"There is a voice that doesn't use words.
Listen." - Rumi*

Why should you connect with your intuition?

Would a runner run a marathon without training? Would the captain of a ship leave without his/her compass? Would you bake a cake without ingredients?

Then why would most of us try to navigate through life without connecting to our inner guidance system?

I think most of us don't realize we can even develop our gifts, or have been taught that this invisible muscle does not exist, is only for special people, or believing in it is considered taboo. Regardless, of these discrepancies, many are starting to experience a type of awareness or awakening or, perhaps, have hit rock bottom and decided to look within for that last glimmer of hope.

Through my journey, I was a seemingly "normal" person going through the motions of society and came full circle to being fully aware of my guides, angels, ability to tap into source to help others, and my life's true purpose. Part of my purpose is guiding others down this same path, so that they can live their lives more fully.

Here is a quiz I share with my newest students to show them how we actually use our gifts on a daily basis and how some of the daily things we pay attention to or experience are actually us using that aspect of our gift.

Clairvoyant (Seer) -

- Do you find yourself daydreaming a lot?
- Did or do you have an imaginary friend?
- Do you experience déjà vu?
- Do you have vivid and in detail dreams?
- Have you ever dreamed something and it came true?
- Can you see ghosts?
- Do you visually imagine what someone's life is like or the people around them?

Clairaudience (Hearer) -

- Do you love listening to music?
- Do you ever wake up with a song in your head?
- Do you have ideas just POP into your head?
- Do you hear voices or whispers when you are sleeping?
- Do you leave the TV or fan on while you are asleep?

Clairsentience (Feel & Know)

- Do you get strong "gut" feelings and just know something is about to happen?
- Do you walk into a room or place and "know" the history?
- Can you sense when someone walks into a room?
- Can pick up information off of objects?

Empathic (Know and FEEL deeply) -

- Do you take on other's problems as your own?
- Do you have to "fix" things so people will be happy?
- Are you sensitive to how others feel without being told?
- Can you spot when someone is lying?

Medium (Speaks to passed loved ones, angels, guides, etc.) -

- Do you have anxiety in large places or groups?
- Do you experience depression upon waking?
- Have you been diagnosed Bipolar?
- Do you have an Auto immune disease?
- Can you see, feel, or hear spirits?

- Do you experience paranormal activity on regular basis?
- Are you scared to be alone at night?
- Can you see, hear, feel or know a presence is near?

These may all sound so normal you may be in disbelief, but it is how I can tell what gift is the strongest with my clients before I start working with them.

Another neat way is to pay attention to the words you use.

You look like the type of person who could.... (clairvoyance)

I know a guy like you who is great at... (claircognizance)

You sound like the type of person who could... (clairaudience)

You feel like the type of person who could... (clairsentience/empathy)

The words you use on a regular basis reveal the strongest aspect of your intuition, and that is where I would suggest focusing on most and what will develop the quickest.

Now that we have the why and what out of the way let me share with you how this book is laid out and what the best approach to take is.

Even though the juicy stuff starts with the hands on exercises and experiences, I am led to share the foundation of intuition development first and foremost. I mean you don't want to eat the fruit before it is ripe, even though you look forward to it. You have to wait! You will be glad you did, and you will understand why the foundation is important once we get through it. I recommend reading through the foundation to get an idea and then applying it during the remainder of the book and your development.

Once you get into the chapters on the "clairs" where you will find exercises, I recommend you stick to one clair per week and work on the exercises for that clair every day that week. If you are like me, I can't wait to read the good stuff nor do I like someone telling me how and what to do (I wish books could have emojis because I'd put the laughing/crying face here), but seriously, go ahead and read the whole thing if you want and THEN come back and focus solely on one at a time. Trust me, this is how I've seen the best results.

So here we go! I'm so glad that you were led to this book. There is no such thing as coincidence and so here is your chance to reconnect, see what special gift you came equipped with, how it can serve your life now, and lead you to find true life purpose and happiness. That is my intention for you!

Chapter 2: Intention

"Our intention creates our reality."

- Wayne Dyer

What is intention and what does it have to do with intuition? For me, I like to refer to intention as the "magic wand." You see, setting an intention is like putting a power booster behind a thought or a goal. It tells the Universe exactly WHY you are doing or asking for something. I like how Deepak describes it here:

> *"What is intention? Intention is a thought, a thing that has a purpose, aim or plan. It's tapping into our mind for a higher purpose, an aim a plan. We have the power within us to use our minds for a higher purpose! Each and everyday thousands of thoughts randomly pass through our mind, most we don't think too much of, however when we make the conscious decision to put purpose behind your thought, we set out a powerful vibration of manifestation into the universe. To*

have intent is to make a decision to purposefully think a thought that has aim and direction."

- Deepak Chopkra

So, for the purpose of developing your intuition, you will be using the power of intention repeatedly. When you want to meet your spiritual team, set an intention. You can say something like I intend that I am ready to meet my spirit guides. When you decide to meditate, set an intention as to why you are meditating. Is it to meet your guides, clean your chakras, receive a download from the angles, or to simply relax and release stress? Set the intention! When you want to see behind a door using your third eye, set an intention that you will receive information about what is behind the door. If you want to do a health scan on a client, set the intention. If you want to find the perfect parking spot, set the intention.

Intention can and should be used for all areas of your life that you want to move energy towards your goal so I have to share with you five steps to creating a powerful intention. You can even use intentions as affirmations by setting an intention for something that you want to bring into your life. Cool, right? Here we go.

1. **I AM!** Always use the words I am because whatever comes after those words is a powerful statement and sends a strong message to your subconscious mind as to what exactly you ARE! Do NOT use words like I wish, I hope, want, need, etc.

2. **Use the present tense.** When you make a statement as if it is already happening it tells your subconscious to figure out a way to make it true.

3. **Use a verb.** When you add a verb it makes your brain visualize the action. For example, I am smelling a flower. You probably just imagined yourself smelling a flower, right? You see your brain doesn't know the difference between a real or a made up memory. It actually does what it would be doing if you were actually smelling the flower. So add in some juicy verbs with your intention to make it that much more real!

4. **Feel your emotions** and how they will be when whatever you are intending manifests. For example, if you are intending to drive a new Blue Tahoe through the mountains, how will you feel then? Really feel the emotion while you make the statement.

5. **Be very specific.** Don't say new red sports car, say 2016 Red Porsche. Don't say a vacation; say exactly where you intend to go. Don't say I intend to have more money. Say how much money. Here is one of my intentions to give you an example. I intend that I am joyfully depositing, investing and being a conduit for $8,500 or better per month consistently. Yeah, the adding on or better is sometimes a great idea too, because the Universe always wants to give us more than we allow for ourselves.

6. **Be present!** Here you are writing these intentions and creating your amazing life and that's great and all but if you don't pay attention you will miss the signs and synchronicities that the Universe is sending. So pay attention and when something or someone comes along with a clue for your next

step to take to get closer to the intention you set then take action!

Now that you understand what an intention is and the power behind it, you will also need to take action with what comes about during or after. Intention is the power booster and director, but then comes faith. Faith is you taking action and saying what you experience during that moment. Without the action, there will be no movement or learning. I call this "Trusting and Allowing." No matter what comes to you, you MUST trust enough to allow it to come out of your mouth when developing your intuition. If you feel like there is a giant pink elephant behind a door, then you MUST say it. If you do NOT take action on what is presented to you then Spirit will stop presenting you with information. If you knew your friend was at home but that she will never answer the door, then you would probably stop knocking or even coming over for that matter.

Trust and allow! I always tease my students and say they need to tattoo those words on their foreheads.

Chapter 3: Journaling

"Journaling is like whispering to one's self and listening at the same time."

- Mina Murray, Dracula

There are many reasons why journaling is a good practice. If you have never tried it, I recommend just letting it all flow. There is no wrong or right way to journal. Most authors use their journals to create their books, including me! It is a safe place to write down our thoughts and emotions to get the weight off. Some people start their day out by journaling about what is bothering them, and what is going great. Others like to keep track of dreams or simply all the random things that happen during daily life.

In developing your intuition, I like to tell my students to journal, journal, journal! And guess what? You there, yes you, the one reading this book. You now have your first homework assignment. The minute you set the intention that you want to develop this invisible gift, all of the Universe moves energy on your behalf. As soon as they sign up for my online development courses, the majority of my students will start experiencing things in relation to their re-awakening that is important to journal. Things such as wild dreams, synchronicities, strange feelings in your stomach, strange knowings, emotional experiences like toxic people falling away, or even strange food cravings or dislikes, are all important to document during your journey. Journal all about it and make sure to date it because things may come together or make more sense at a later date and then you have somewhere to come back to and reference it.

When you set out to meet your spirit guides, they like to see you journal what your experience was. Journaling is a form of communicating with them. If your guides show you or tell you something in a meditation and then you journal about it, they will know you received the information. And if you journal but leave some key points out then that is a sign to your guides to deliver the message again or for them to try using a different approach or different form of communication.

Another benefit of journaling is that it brings your thoughts from your head (non-physical) onto the paper (psychical realm). It is the first step in manifesting. For example, writing down questions in your journal is an invitation to the Universe to lead you to the answer. Writing in your journal versus letting our brain keep track, will keep the information fresh. in plain sight, puts power to it and gets the ball rolling.

Additionally, your re-awakening process and your experiences may lead to that book you've always wanted to write. Your spiritual team has a lot to say, not just to you, but to all of humanity and many gifted people use their journal and end up channeling via automatic writing.

When should you journal? The best time to journal is after being in a meditative state when your mind is still and aware. That is when you are closest to consciousness and can receive what many call "downloads." I also recommend journaling after waking up from a vivid dream; when you are upset; journal about your goals and what you want more of in your life. Of course, when you have an "aha" moment grab that journal, because that "aha" moment is most likely inspiration! And I read somewhere that the word *inspiration* can mean in-spirit.

If you haven't heard me say this yet, trust and allow what comes to you enough to write it down. So grab your pen and your journal and just free write something today! Get into the habit and watch how things start unfolding.

Chapter 4: Meditation

"Meditation is listening to the divine within."

- Edgar Cayce

Meditation! Yeah, you know, quieting the brain! I was like most people when introduced to meditation, and I thought, "Yeah right, I've got a party going on in my head how will I make it stop and be quiet?" At first, I felt like running for the hills because I thought that I would have to be "monk-like" to achieve this state of nirvana, but I promise that isn't the case. Just 15 minutes a day got me going on the right path, and that is what I recommend for you.

Meditation is not about silencing your mind chatter but rather witnessing it without judgment. Once you catch yourself thinking about what is for dinner, just go back to the practice. The easiest way I found to start out with meditation is to do deep breaths in and out, all the while the only thing I would think of is "I am breathing in, I am breathing out, I am breathing in, I am breathing out". After some practice, I found that I reached a point of "nothingness" where nothing exists but you and your breath.

It was so worth it for me because, after a couple of times, I noticed that I would come back to this real life, feeling refreshed, at peace, not a worry in the world. For me, even 5 minutes of not worrying or trying to control life, makes me feel good. Meditating on a regular basis can achieve this for you as well as countless other experiences including waking up your intuition.

The more often and the more regular I would meditate, the faster I started finding peace in all situations. I witnessed myself not reacting like I used to in stressful situations, and I saw the chaos around me as it "just is" with no emotion. It just IS.

Protection

Although you wouldn't think that sitting still and meditating would require protection, you do tend to be open to all energy that is around you. Additionally, since we will be meeting guides and other beings that are "out there," it is a good idea to imagine a white light around you before starting and setting an intention to only experience love and light. Simply imagine a white light that is close to your skin as if you had put on a white bath robe. This light will keep any negative energy away from you during your practice. Just remember you are in charge, and there is nothing to fear. You can also ask your angels, guides, and past loved ones to protect you during meditation and even if you don't know who your guides and angels are, trust me, they will help you out.

Meditation Exercise 1:

Here are a few other simple meditation techniques that I recommend you try for yourself. Give yourself at least two weeks of trying this and I believe you will witness the feeling I describe. Make sure to journal your experiences.

The Breath: The breath is, I think, the best place to start with meditation. It is always there for you, even when you're not meditating, and is a very useful way to develop attention in this simple activity in the present moment. You can direct your awareness to the sensation of air passing at the tip of your nose, or the expansion of your belly, whichever is easiest for you to notice and follow. Be aware of the in-breath, through the entire duration of the inhale, and then switch to the out-breath until its completion. Then invite the attention as fresh with the next breath, and the one after that, just observing the sensation. It is completely normal to get lost and catch yourself thinking random thoughts. It is okay, just resume back to meditation. Allow the thought to pass and just take notice without emotion and then go back to the breath.

Feel your body parts. A great practice for beginning meditators is to take notice of the body when a meditative state starts to take hold. Once the mind quiets, put all your attention on the feet and then slowly move your way up the body (include your internal organs). This simple awareness is very healthy and an indicator that you are on the right path.

Find peace during stressful times. Meditation doesn't always have to be a formal event. If you get irritated, by all means, retreat to a quiet spot, preferably outdoors, and do some deep breathing until you find you are grounded again.

Make it a time when you know that you will not be interrupted. If you know you have a phone call coming in soon, you will not be able to focus on the mediation.

Listen to guided meditations or have relaxing music play to keep you focused.

Open eyes technique. While this may sound like an advanced technique, it can be very helpful for beginners because having your eyes closed seems to let the mind race to look for what's not there. With the open eyes technique, you want to stay focused on an item or area and just keep watching your mind and the thoughts arise. Once a thought comes, just acknowledge it and then go back to focusing on the item you've selected. It could be a leaf on a tree, a gazing ball, a flower or a lit candle.

Some meditations are just to ground down, re-center yourself, and be in the "void", in the nothingness, and some meditations are for a purpose with an intent behind them, such as meeting your Spirit Guides, or feeling love around you, etc. Once you get the hang of meditation then you can use it for many different reasons. You can do it to de-stress, relax, meet your guides, clean your chakras and body's energy centers, heal your body, and many more reasons and techniques.

Meditation Exercise 2:

A great meditation exercise is to watch the mind move and to witness that your thoughts aren't even made up by you. The first time I heard that I thought my teacher was crazy, but she's right. If you knew what you were going to think about in 5 minutes from now, you would seemingly have control over your thoughts, but guess what, you have no idea what your brain will be coming up within 5 minutes. So watch the mind chatter. Watch what it worries about, watch what it judges you for, and watch how it scolds you, or speaks unkindly about others or even yourself. Remember, don't judge the thoughts or get frustrated when they come up while you are trying to be still. They just are thoughts; no emotion needs to be associated with it. Witness the thought and go back to the breath or whatever form of practice you are using.

It is in this meditation practice that you will come to notice how your own thoughts have allowed limitations to become beliefs. It is then that you will see the ego working to keep you in that still small space, away from happiness and to keep control over you. It is when we witness this, that we can make changes and remove cellular synopsis. So the next time you smell roses, you won't be reminded of "whatever" happened the first time you smelled roses. You can break the habit and train your brain to change your life for the better.

I invite you to listen to a couple of guided meditations I have on my website to assist you in grounding down, chakra cleansing, and more. Just go to the resource section on my website at **brandaleen.com/resources.html** for your free meditations.

Chapter 5: Raise your vibration.

When developing your intuition, it is important and beneficial to raise your vibration. I love that this book is being drafted at the same time I am working with a client and friend who is writing her very own book that is specifically on the subject of raising your vibration. Here is a quote from her book, "Spirit Crack" to start off this chapter.

"Reasons why you should raise your vibration:

The Universe and our planet are made up of ENERGY! Everything we see is ENERGY! You are made of ENERGY, so are the birds in sky, the plants and even places. VIBRATIONS ARE THE MEASUREMENT OF ENERGY. We all have different energy levels depending on our emotions, humor, states of health, etc. Depending on how high your VIBRATION is, the easier it is to manifest whatever it is that you desire! This energy circulates through our 7 chakra centers. Being aware of your vibes at every moment is the key to a much happier life and obtaining everything you desire.

Raise your vibration, and the earth and your reality will positively change with you.

More creativity!

Overcome negative thoughts.

Heal your body. Come into immaculate health.

Decrease anxiety and depression.

Strengthen your mental skills.

Design yourself! Yup, you can design every inch of your life. Inside and out.

NOBODY is going to save you. Learn to save yourself!"

    -Sky Wonders

In my development courses, I like to explain it to my students like this. You probably have a television in your house and that television is open to receive information. Some people have high-speed cable; some have satellite, and some only use a simple antenna. Still, some others purchase televisions that have the capability to have a super clear picture such as high definition, etc. The point I am making is your connection to source energy is affected by how high or low your vibration is and how clean or toxic your body is. Both your body, physical and ethereal, and your vibrations are tools that spirit uses to transfer the information from. So having a low vibration and a toxic body (which go hand in hand) is like having an old black and white T.V. with tiny rabbit ears (that's an old school antenna for you young peeps).

So how can you raise your vibration? Raising your vibration can be done in each aspect of your life by working with physical, mental, emotional and spiritual practices. Here are some examples:

- Singing
- Meditation
- Yoga

- Drinking pure water
- Detoxing from heavy metals and toxins.
- Being in sunshine
- Grounding
- Being outside in nature
- Balancing and cleansing your chakras
- Energy work such as reiki, massage or the like
- Submerging yourself in salt water
- Changing to a vegetarian or raw vegan diet
- Staying positive
- Essential oils
- And so much more.

Even your spiritual team members, your guides, angels and loved ones, are on the other side helping with this because they know the higher your vibration, the easier it is for you to receive their messages and the clearer they will be.

Chakras

While this book doesn't go into great detail on the chakra system, I feel it is an important system to understand so you can work with each area of your physical, mental, emotional and spiritual health in regards to chakras. There are several books on chakras. Let your intuition guide you to the one that will be most helpful to your personal frequency.

Chakras are your body's main energy centers that bring energy into various areas of the body. We have seven main chakras and multiple minor chakras. We also have chakras above and below our head and feet reaching into different dimensions. Yeah, it goes deep.

Each chakra represents an aspect of your spiritual, emotional, physical, and mental health. If your chakra is out of balance or blocked, it may lead to dis-ease in that area of your body/life. When you develop your intuition, you will receive information from Spirit/Source through your chakra system, into your physical body and then out of your mouth, therefore, having your chakra system clean and vibrating at a high frequency will affect the quality of your connection.

Ways to clean your chakras and/or balance them are: Energy work such as Reiki; body work such as massage and yoga, visualizations like breathing in the corresponding color and imagining it swirl clockwise, wearing the corresponding color, eating the corresponding food color, working with gemstones of the corresponding color, etc.

Below is very basic information on each chakra, such as what color each chakra is, where it is at on the body, and what that chakra represents in the spiritual, emotional, physical, and mental areas.

Root chakra. The root chakra is located at the base of the spine and is the color red. This chakras function is on survival, feeling secure and safe, grounding, stability, courage, etc.

Having an under-active root chakra causes fear or worry about money, stability, feeling lack, etc. Having an over active root chakra would cause obsession over money and material items.

Sacral chakra. The sacral chakra is located in the center of the abdomen below the belly button and is the color orange. The function of the sacral chakra is personal desires, primal feelings, sexuality, enthusiasm, and creativity.

Having an under-active sacral chakra causes worry and stress about the physical body (weight, health, appearance) and an overactive sacral chakra causes an obsession with the body, cravings, and addictions.

Solar plexus chakra. The solar plexus chakra is located above the belly button and below the chest and is the color yellow. The function of this chakra is personal power, social identity, influence, self-control, energy, peace radiance, joy, vitality and inner strength.

Having an under-active solar plexus chakra causes fear of losing control and fear of being controlled. An overactive solar plexus chakra causes obsession of being in control and gaining power over others.

Heart chakra. The heart chakra is located at the center of the chest. This chakra is the color green but pink is also associated with this chakra. The function of this chakra is love, relationships, passion, joy, and feeling connected.

An under-active heart chakra causes fear of rejection, hate, jealousy, isolation, and disbelief in unconditional love. A balanced heart chakra allows you to feel deep love for others, connected to others, open to love and accepting others, joy, and peace.

Throat chakra. The throat chakra is located in the throat and is the color blue. The function of the throat chakra is communication, expression, inspiration, wisdom, confidence, and self-expression through music, art, writing, etc.

If the throat chakra is under-active, one would have a fear of expressing themselves. If it is overactive, one would be obsessive in communicating, talking to hear themselves.

Third eye chakra. The third eye chakra probably gets the most attention when working with intuition, because the primary function of this chakra is intuition, psychic abilities, visualization, dreams, memory, and comprehension. This chakra is located in the middle of the forehead and is the color purple/indigo.

If this chakra is out of balance, it may cause joint problems, dehydration, fertility issues, and isolation and guilt.

When this chakra is in balance, it can cause fertility, joy, creativity, adaptability, and going with the flow of life.

Crown chakra. The crown chakra is located at the top of the head and is the color violet. The function of this chakra is claircognizance, unity with the divine, wisdom and purpose, universal consciousness, and enlightenment.

Chakra exercises:

I always have my students spend time with their chakras for at least a week. I have them meditate and not only feel their chakras but draw them, are they spinning properly, do they feel too open or shut down? Just let your intuitive knowing guide you. You can also talk to your chakra and ask it what it wants. This may sound crazy, but they will send you some type of message.

Another great exercise I did actually to feel my chakras open and close was sat quietly and felt angry. Pay attention to how your body reacts to feeling angry. Can you feel your solar plexus and sacral chakras close? Now feel joyful and hold that feeling while you do the same exercise. Go ahead and practice feeling different emotions and how those emotions affect your chakra system. It will be a real eye opener as to how important it is to stay in a joyful state of mind.

Chapter 6: Pineal Gland, the Seat to your Soul

"Keep the pineal gland clean and you won't grow old-you will always be young."

- *Edgar Cayce*

What is a pineal gland and what the heck does it have to do with developing intuition and mediumship?

The actual definition is:

"A pea-sized conical mass of tissue behind the third ventricle of the brain, secreting a hormone-like substance in some mammals."

This tiny organ regulates your daily and seasonal circadian rhythms, the sleep-wake patterns that determine your hormone levels, stress levels, and physical performance. It produces melatonin, a hormone that affects the modulation of wake/sleep patterns and photoperiodic (seasonal) functions. Located near to the center of the brain between the two hemispheres, it looks like a tiny pine cone, hence its name.

Ok, that sounds like medical jargon to me too, but what ELSE does it do? I'm not sure where to find scientific information, but the famous philosopher Descartes described the pineal gland as the "principal seat of the soul." What I've come to understand is that this tiny gland that looks like a cute little pine cone is our connection to all that is, all of creation, all dimensions, and all of consciousness. When it is activated, we may have the ability to remote view, astral travel and connect to other dimensions, as well as have the knowing of what we are experiencing while we are doing it. Yeah, it's freaking amazing, right?

So why aren't we all levitating and flying through the cosmos if we have this gland? It is because most of us have what is called a calcified pineal gland, which prevents this sweet tool of ONENESS from doing what it does best, keeping us connected and our gifts turned on!

What causes our pineal gland to become calcified? In the late 90's, a scientist by the name of Jennifer Luke carried out the first study on the effects of sodium fluoride on the pineal gland. She determined that the pineal gland, located in the middle of the brain, was a target for fluoride. The pineal gland simply absorbed more fluoride than any other physical matter in the body, even bones!

The pineal gland is unprotected by the blood brain barrier (the protective sheath that keeps crap in your blood from entering your cerebrospinal fluid). As a result, whatever toxins we have floating around in our blood stream, be it calcium, fluoride, or other nasty crud, waltz right in and become sludge in your pineal gland.

Another interesting thing I read about sodium fluoride is that it becomes a magnet for heavy metals and therefore any heavy metals you have in our system, goes to the pineal gland just as fast as chocolate lands on your hips! Sodium fluoride is in our water, our food, soda, and personal care products. We become dumbed down and are complacent, meaning we become unconcerned with things that we should concern us. We essentially become "sheeple," if you have heard that phrase before.

For a healthy pineal gland, you may want to detoxify it to decalcify it. The first thing you may want to do is **stop consuming fluoride**. You will be amazed when you educate yourself how many places you will find fluoride. I am super passionate about removing heavy metals from our diets, our products, and even our clothing has been found to have heavy metals in it! Adding in supplements to your diet such as turmeric, spirulina, chlorella, eating greens (cilantro is a great herb to pull heavy metals), and omega 3s will help pull the toxins from your system.

How to help activate your pineal gland:

Meditation is hands down the most important way to activate your pineal gland. When we meditate, regardless if your gland is calcified, we are using and exercising our pineal gland. Adding in the mantra "Om" as part of your meditation practice will also stimulate your pineal gland.

Being in the sunshine or even sun gazing is said to infuse energy literally into cells throughout our body. Please research sun gazing before you attempt it as the human eye is very sensitive, and it can cause health problems.

Sleep in the dark. Because our pineal gland is the regulator of our sleep patterns, it is sensitive to light, and a good idea to make sure you are getting enough sleep is to keep that sleeping gland asleep!

With a clean and active pineal gland, this quote will ring true to you, because you will no longer be dumbed down or complacent and will see through many illusions that society as a whole has believed to be true. With that my friends, I'll just leave you with this quote from Buddha!

"Do not believe in anything simply because you have heard it. Do not believe in anything simply because it is spoken and rumored by many. Do not believe in anything simply because it is found written in your religious books. Do not believe in anything merely on the authority of your teachers and elders. Do not believe in traditions because they have been handed down for many generations. But after observation and analysis, when you find that anything agrees with reason and is conducive to the good and benefit of one and all, then accept it and live up to it."

-Buddha

Chapter 7: Self-Care

*"Self-care is not about self-indulgence,
it's about self = preservation."*

- Audrey Lord

Along with the previous chapter on raising your vibration, self-care is crucial for the sensitive person. You will probably agree with me when I say that self-care is likely to be last on the list for the majority of people regardless if they are developing their inner guidance system or not, right? So any sensitive person working with the invisible realms will have to be disciplined in making it a priority. As a matter of fact, self-care is a form of protection if you ask me, especially when dealing with the invisible realm. You want to keep your energy field clean and vibrant in when working with your intuition. What you vibrate at, you attract. Remember, we only work with love and light only.

Self-care obviously has to do with being healthy, right? But it also means to educate yourself about what you put on, in, or around your body. This includes the type of people you allow around you.

Some things I share in my development classes regarding self-care are:

Information about the dangers of Wi-Fi and electronic devices and the effects it has on our pineal gland (3rd eye), our brain waves and our energy field: Let me just state here the effects are not good! Go ahead and fire up Google and see for yourself. In this day and age, yes, we need our Wi-Fi and electronic devices. So what I do is take the best precautions I can. At my house, we turn off the Wi-Fi at night or when we aren't using it. We leave our cellular phones in the kitchen where we can still hear them if someone is calling but far away enough to not disrupt our sleep patterns.

Self-care products: What is inside the products you currently use? I have replaced my shampoo, conditioner, deodorant, lotion, and toothpaste all with using coconut oil and baking soda. I like to share that we should use what our great-grandparents used (or great-great-grandparents depending your age). Please take some time and educate yourself on this!

Energy vampires: This is for real, and you will, or already have, think of someone on your friends or family roster that is one, once I describe them. An energy vampire is someone who, even sometimes unbeknownst to themselves, creates drama of some sort for the purpose of hooking you in to steal your valuable energy. They will be nice at first. That is the way they lure you in and then BAM, they will belittle you, talk about you to someone else, and let you find out on purpose, or create drama in some way to get you riled up. Once that happens, the energy exchange has started. You will be left feeling angry, betrayed, and drained while they feel empowered and refreshed from stealing your energy. I like to describe them as a two-year-old having a tantrum in the mall. If you give in to the two-year-old and give them a sucker to keep them quiet then you have taught the child that it will receive a reward for its behavior, right? The next time the child has a tantrum; it will escalate even further than the last time because it knows a sucker is in its future. For those of you that have an energy vampire, it is imperative to cut them off of their energy source, meaning you! They may very well create a large "tantrum," if you will, once you cut them off. They are used to manipulating you and won't be happy with the energetic loss. I had my own experience in this with one being my first husband and the second being my brother-in-law. They both about lost their minds after I wised up and cut the cords, and this is exactly what you need to do. One last note is that an energy vampire and a narcissist go hand in hand.

Best wishes in your vampire slaying.

Self-care exercise:

Sit with your spirit guides in a meditation and ask them to tell you what one thing should you do, or stop doing in regards to your self-care. They may give you something, you may have a knowing, even if you don't receive it in the meditation, you may open Facebook and see a post on self-care or get an e-mail from a friend asking you to go to yoga with her. Be present, grounded, and on the lookout for synchronicity to strike after this exercise. Whatever it is that they show you, it is important to honor their guidance and take action to do so. It's for your highest good after all.

Time for just you! If you are reading this book, then I already know (because I am psychic) that you care deeply for others. You probably put yourself last and would help a stranger. Once your gifts have developed, you will have the ability to help even more people than you already do and you will also be attracting people that need guidance and will seek you out and want it all for free. First, I'm here to tell you don't do it! You will be sucked dry trying to help everyone who crosses your path, and your field will drain. I'm sharing from experience. One time my husband said to me, "You don't even have time for your business to grow because you are constantly helping people, and even I don't get time with you!" Make it a point to always, always get an energy exchange for your services. Of course, Spirit will send you people, and you will know when it is appropriate to give a service for free, yes, but the other 99% of the time you need an energy exchange! An energy exchange can be money, a trade for the same price of service, a review on your business page, a plate of cookies, etc. Secondly, take time each week to focus on you and time alone with yourself. Read a book, drink herbal tea, get a massage. No excuses, love yourself every week!

Chapter 8: Protection

"If you are feeling scared or vulnerable call on Archangel Michael and ask him to give you courage and protection to help you through."

- Unknown

Protection? Why? Because everything, and I do mean everything, is energy, and some energy isn't all Love and Light. This energy can even be from energy vampires (explained below), screaming children, argumentative words or just negative energy in general. There isn't anything to fear, but it is a smart idea to protect yourself from anything less than positive vibes.

Basic protection shield: Imagine yourself covered with a bright white light. It is like a robe on you and touching your skin. Nothing can penetrate this light. Imagine that same light washing over you and washing away any energy that may have gotten stuck on you. This technique should be used before meditation, when you get out of bed, and anytime you are going to work with spirit, energy, etc.

How energy gets stuck on you. During the day you have interactions with people, and each interaction creates a sort of energy attachment (cording) from you to the person and vice versa. It is important to our health that we are operating with only our energy and not let other energies pull from ours. When a psychic medium connects with the dead or even a living client, they are literally inside their energy field regardless of location. This creates a cord and is important to "wash away" the energy. If you don't wash it away, you will continue to think randomly about the reading or the client's well-being, etc. because you are essentially still connected.

Some cords can be created even by worrying about a family member which has you unknowingly sending them your energy and can leave you feeling drained. Another example of cording is what I call energy vampires. Many of us have a particular person that we do not feel comfortable being around. It can even be a family member that creates drama or as simple as a 2-year-old throwing a tantrum that creates a 'hook' into our energy field and starts draining us. Energy vampires are often very controlling and can turn a pleasant situation into a dramatic moment.

Cutting Cords Technique: I cut cords after all of my readings and also each day as part of my meditation. To cut cords imagine a white waterfall washing over you washing away any attachments, energy, and cords you may have from other people, situations, and spirits. For stronger cord cutting technique, ask Archangel Michael to come in and cut cords for you. Michael is your main man when it comes to asking for any protection, and I will be talking about him later in this book as well.

Chakra Cleaning: To clean your chakras, I recommend breathing in the corresponding chakra color and imagining the color swirling in a clockwise motion at its destination, i.e. red for your root chakra, etc. Once you have done this for all seven main chakras, then you imagine flossing them. You imagine the brightest white light as a piece of floss and pull it through each chakra. You may notice specs or chunks fly off and send them to the white light.

Smudging/saging your personal spaces: Negative energy can get stuck in all the nooks and crannies of your home, office or even car, so it is important to clean your spaces on a regular basis. If you work with spirit, I recommend at least once a week for your home and office. I sage my home office after every reading and the entire house once a week. There are several different types of sage so pick what you want and wave that bad boy around. Get the closets, in the shower, under the bed, etc. Your front door should always be open during this so that the negative energy can get out versus pushing it from room to room. It is best to air out your house on a regular basis as well so the more doors and windows open, the better.

Sea Salt: Sea salt is an excellent neutralizer! The ocean holds a lot of power, especially for cleansing and healing, so sea salt obviously does too. You can get pure sea salt at health food stores, the regular grocery store and many online shops also carry it. Try to get "unrefined sea salt" if possible, because it retains most of its natural properties. You can mix in some sea salt with your herb mixtures, put it in a bowl on the floor to collect the negative energy, scrub your body in the shower to ionize yourself or soak in it in the tub. You can also put most crystals in sea salt to clean them.

Crystals: You can wear protective crystals while you work with energies. Black Tourmaline, Rose Quartz, Amethyst, and Turquoise are just a few that offer protective qualities. Just pick out the one that stands out to you. I have small black tourmaline pieces in the four corners of my home, my office and my bedroom as a protection grid. I can tell a difference in how the energy feels since doing so.

Grounding

Symptoms of being ungrounded

- Feeling spaced out or like you have ADHD
- Excessive worrying
- Can't complete tasks
- aches and pains
- Anxiousness

When working with your intuition, you are often operating with the top four chakras and are open to receive information from higher realms. This can leave you feeling spaced out, nervous, anxious, and worrisome.

After you do any intuitive work, it is important to ground.

Ways to ground down outside

- Stand outside barefoot
- Sit with your back to a tree
- Go for a walk
- Go to the beach – feet in sand
- Spend time in nature – appreciate it

Ways to ground down inside

- Take a sea salt bath
- Visualize roots coming from you going to the core of mother earth

- Breath in through your feet
- Lay flat on your back
- Smack the bottom of your feet
- Wear grounding stones
- Have sex
- Brush your dog/animal

Health Benefits of Grounding

Inflammation reduction

Shields us from electromagnetic energy. I like to describe this as sort of a windshield. If your car doesn't have a windshield, you will most likely end up being pelted with bugs. With a windshield in place those bugs, or harmful electromagnetic energy, actually flow around you.

Slows aging process by being one of our greatest sources of antioxidants.

Neutralizes the positive forces on the body (free radicals and electromagnetic fields)

Once the connection is made, an instantaneous flow of free electrons enters the body.

I remember reading that when someone is not grounded, free radicals "steal" electrons from other healthy atoms to stabilize. As a result of this process, a new free radical is therefore created, perpetuating a snowball effect. In essence, this is what ages us, eek!

Boundaries: I saved this one for last because this is where it starts to get juicy. :) Bear with me as I start to sound crazy to some or it may have you going OH MY GOSH, no wonder!!!

Boundaries are your rules. These rules are for Spirit Guides, Angels, passed loved ones, and any energies that you may not be aware of, need to follow. It is kind of like an invisible dog fence. You know how they bury the invisible shield, and the dogs learn that they cannot cross over that boundary? Well, this is your invisible spirit fence.

Your list of boundaries should be kept somewhere that you can reference and add to or take away from during your spiritual development. For example, some of you may already have spirits waking you in the middle of the night. You may not know it is them, but suddenly awakening around 2-4 am, especially if it comes along with anxiety, is a telltale sign that someone wants your attention. Even if it is Aunt Matilda stopping by to say hello, we still need our sleep and so an example of this boundary would be writing down in your journal (the physical realm): No spirits are allowed in my bedroom unless I invite them or no spirits are allowed to wake me up. You can add specifics, such as unless there is an emergency, before 6 am, etc., etc. You can be general, but specific may suit you best.

Boundaries can be made for just about everything you don't want, or to specify what you do want or how you feel comfortable in receiving your information. For me, in the beginning, I wrote on my list that I do not want to see actual dead people walking around in my house or public. I also would have peed my pants if I heard an ominous voice calling out my name. You may be thinking, "How do you know if there really is a dead person in your house Brandaleen if you can't see them or hear them?" When I created that boundary, my spiritual team found other ways that were more comfortable for me. I see the dead in my imagination (third eye) only and not with my human eyes lurking around the corner, and as far as hearing, I hear through the thoughts in my head during a reading and not necessarily outside of my head. Although now it wouldn't freak me out to physically hear them, I still don't think I want to hear my name called.

For me when I do see the dead in my imagination I see them dressed in one of their regular outfits and often spirit will show me what they looked like in a photo that one of their living loved one has in their possession. Sometimes one of my students will see them in a way that is uncomfortable for them, such as missing a limb, having their face covered by a mask or may even witness the violence that ensued at their death. These are all great reasons to put on your boundary list. Let spirit know what you don't want! You are the boss of your experience. I can't say this enough.

One thing I've had is a lot of calls from parents saying their child hears voices, has spirit in their room at night, night terrors, and more so I help the parents teach their children to establish boundaries to make their lives easier to live. We can ask to make it stop or ask to make it clearer; these are our rules.

I have listed some of my boundaries here to give you a better idea.

- No one is allowed in my bedroom unless I invite them.
- I prefer to see the dead as they are in a photograph and not after death.
- I don't speak to spirit after 10 (or after two glasses of wine) or before 8 am.

- I do not speak to spirit in public places. (Some love this, I do not).

- I only speak to spirits that are my vibration or higher, or who have a higher vibratory spirit speaking for them.

- No spirits are allowed to get inside my body. I made this one after someone's grandmother was impatient.

Wow, this chapter has a lot of information in it, doesn't it? Hey, I have the hook up for you so you can let it all sink in. Go ahead and pop onto my website and watch the videos I have to go along with this chapter at **brandaleen.com/resources.html**

Chapter 9: Agreements

"Agreements with Spirit is like playing charades with invisible people."

- *Brandaleen Johnson*

Now that you have what I call the foundation to intuition development down, let's go a little deeper. Agreements may be something that comes later for you, but I do want to address it now because some of you probably already have some in place and don't know it. An Agreement is a shortcut to a longer version of information. Just like you have a shortcut to a program on your laptop or an App on your smartphone it is a way to get somewhere or something quickly.

How does spirit (Angels, guides, Goddess, past loved ones, etc.) give us information? They use our brains, our memories, our emotions, past experiences, etc. Each one of us has our very own life experience. If I say the words Mallard Duck, every single one of you has had a different experience, thought, or emotion about that statement. Some may have a fear of ducks, others maybe remember their grandfather feeding them at the park, some it may mean peace, and on and on. Make sense?

So for the purpose of developing your intuition, you will need to pay attention to when you are open to receive information from Spirit and what memories, experiences, emotions, and even sounds and smells show up. Those can all be translated into agreements.

For example, when I first started doing readings, I kept seeing the color purple in my mind's eye with certain people. It wasn't until I discovered that all the people I would see purple with during their reading had something in common that I figured out why. They all had a grandmother in spirit who helps with their spirituality. Right then and there was my agreement with spirit. Now, that is my agreement, not yours or anyone else's. From that moment on, if I see purple, that means I am being prompted to say to the client that their grandmother in spirit is helping them with their spirituality from the other side.

If you watch the *Long Island Medium*, you will notice she says things like, "They are snapping their fingers, and that means someone died suddenly or unexpectedly," or she'll say, "They are showing me a red rose, and that means it is the anniversary of someone's death."

There are a couple of ways you can make agreements. The first is the same way I described above; by trial and error and similarities through experience doing readings. This has been the way my agreements come into place. Here are a few more examples of agreements I have with Spirit. Keep in mind; I am Clairvoyant, and many of my agreements are visual.

Seeing a roller coaster = Client's relationship is on a roller coaster ride.

White = Medical worker, or wedding

Goosebumps = YES, talk more about that or you are spot on.

Sick stomach or pain in the head = Negative energy or client has a negative spirit with them.

Stomach flip flops = Pay attention information is about to come in.

I am also strongly clairsentient. I have agreements with that too, but those are harder for me to describe. I get a certain feeling in my stomach, and it will translate to things like "he is a coach for a living," or "Nashville, TN," or "she lives far away," and on and on. I know it sounds crazy, but that's how I can describe it.

That is just a few, but hopefully, that helps you understand.

The second way I teach my students to make agreements is to sit down and invite their spiritual team members in, in love and light only! Have your journal handy and ask spirit for the specific things you would like shortcuts. When teaching my students, I recommend their agreements be something that they will be working on frequently. So if you are a health worker or in the healing field, you may want to know agreements for health related things. If you want to focus more on relationships, you will want to get those types of agreements.

For example, you may say to spirit: How will I know if someone died suddenly or unexpectedly? How will I know if a wedding is in the future? How will I know if I am on the right track? How will I know if it is the anniversary of a death or a wedding (those would be two agreements)?

Once you make the statement or ask the question, be quiet and wait for something to come. It may be your left foot gets hot; you may see a color, smell a scent, or feel a sensation in your body. You may even taste something. Journal whatever you experience. Next time it is brought to your attention, your job is to trust and allow enough to say to the client what your agreement is.

You do not usually have to ask these questions during a reading; rather the agreement will present itself to you as a sign to mention whatever it is.

You will notice that as time goes on and you have more experience under your belt that new agreements may present themselves or some of your agreements may fall away. In my experience, my clairaudience and claircognizance have overridden many of my agreements because now I just know. Even a few of my students wanted to skip over the agreements because their connection with hearing their spiritual team was substantial from the very beginning.

I still see the roller coasters though, haha, and of course ALWAYS the flip-flopping of the stomach and validation of the goosebumps! Sometimes I feel like a one man band.

Did I mention that I love spirit!? :)

CHAPTER 10: MEET YOUR SPIRIT GUIDES

Be guided by spirit and not driven by ego.

First things first, it is way easier to meet your spiritual team members than you think. Our human brains have told us that this is strange, crazy, made up, our imagination has gone wild, and this couldn't possibly be real.

Repeat after me. It TOTALLY is real! First, I will share about it all and then I will explain how you can prove to yourself that it is truly a real experience.

Our main spirit guide(s) have been with us our entire life. They were with us when we were born and will remain with us until we return. They are extremely familiar to us because we have had many lifetimes together. They are so close to you that they decided to stay behind in this life to guide you, and you have, or will, do the same for them. Just the fact that they are so familiar to us is why so many of us overlook their presence and their daily reminders and signs that they are truly living our lives with us. Hey, who doesn't want a whole team leading them towards a freaking amazing life? I know I do!

You may have seen them in your dreams (a protector during nightmares). When I was younger, anytime I had a nightmare

I could look back to my right, and a blonde lady was there. Whenever I saw her, I knew I would be alright and that it was just a nightmare.

You may collect things that they have been showing you for your entire life and not know it. I have several items with a particular swirly design on them - from plates to clothes, to bedding, to collectibles. They ALL have the same swirly design on them. Hey, I figured I just loved swirlies but when I first met my guide that is the same design she has on her outfit as well as seeing that same swirl in many other meditations. Coincidence? Never.

Another thing you may collect is things like butterflies, gnomes, turtle figurines, whatever you collect there is a meaning to it. If you love something enough to have a tattoo of it, then you have a connection. Most of the time these end up to be totem or spirit animals. I like to look them up on this site for the meaning.

(http://www.spirit-animals.com/spirit-animal-totem/)

You may remember having an imaginary friend as a child. This is a perfect telltale sign that you had a connection with your guide earlier in life!

You may collect inanimate objects and feel they have meaning to you or even have spirits inside them. Sounds crazy, right? But as crazy as it sounds, I have heard and experienced these things to be true during my spiritual journey of teaching so many to reconnect.

When you go to meet your guide, it will feel just like home. No, a giant alien won't be jumping out at you. Your guides want you to open up, awaken to your life's full potential and happiness, so the last thing they are going to do is show up as something frightening. If you are really into Jesus and the bible, then you may have Jesus show up as a guide. I have seen this on many occasions. If you are very mystical and into fairies and Celtic, then you may have a dragon or a tree person. It will fit into your genre so to speak. <u>It feels normal because it is YOUR normal.</u>

Lastly, before we dive into actually meeting your guide(s), I am clairvoyant, so my strongest gift to start with is 'seeing' with my mind's eye. Therefore, I could see my guides before I could hear them or before I could feel them. This is just me, not you, so do not judge how you meet your team member(s). You may not see them, just feel them. You may not feel them but hear them, etc. The biggest thing here is for you to allow and trust the process. Remember, trust and allow should be your favorite words during your spiritual awakening.

Let's meet our guides!

First, protect your energy using the techniques described in the chapter on protection. Invite in your guides in love and light only. Ask them to be very clear and to raise your vibration to help you perceive their higher energy. I recommend you read through the text of this guided meditation and then go back and actually do it.

Take a couple of deep breaths and close your eyes. Imagine your favorite place in nature. Look around yourself. What do you see? Notice how you feel. Do you feel a breeze? Is it day or night? Are you wearing shoes? Is it warm or cool? Do you hear any nature sounds? Become aware of where you are.

Smile today because you are going to meet your guide(s). Off to the distance, you see a pathway and decide to walk down it. Towards the end of the pathway, you can see large rocks formed into a type of circle. Walk towards them. Notice what the ground feels like under your feet. Look to the left and right of the pathway and admire what you see. You are feeling so peaceful and happy to be in your favorite spot. You come closer to the large rocks, and you decide to sit on one. What color is it? How does it feel to the touch? Sit down and take a deep breath. You notice a beautiful glowing light coming from your solar plexus area. It is bright and yellow and warm. It grows bigger and envelopes you.

You decide to write on a piece of paper you have in your hand. You write "I am now ready to meet my guide." Then you toss the paper into the middle of the rock circle and wait. Maybe you see someone approach, or maybe you just feel a sense of a male or female energy. You are safe and comfortable and maybe a bit excited to be reunited. Ask your guide to sit with you.

Don't try to see more than you see, or feel more than you feel. Don't judge your experience. Just know that your guide is with you and sit with him/her for a moment.

Now I want you to ask your guide, "What is your name?" Just allow something to come, don't try. Thank them.

Now ask your guide, why are you here to guide me? What is your purpose? Maybe you have a knowing already. Thank them.

Your guide is so happy that you came to meet him/her that your guide has a gift for you. Open your hand and accept this gift. Thank your guide for being with you today. Thank your guide for being with you always. Now let your guide return to where he/she came from and send love!

Now you can walk back down that pathway back to your favorite spot in gratitude for what you just experienced. You can now come back into this room and back into your body. Take a couple of breaths and open your eyes slightly. Keep this feeling for a moment. You don't need to jump back into regular life yet. **Go ahead and journal down everything you experienced.**

This is the part where you feel surreal for a minute, and then the ego jumps in telling you that you made all that up. Lock the ego in the bathroom for a minute, and let's get validation!! So many of my students say to me, "I think my guide said his name was Adam but then maybe he said Arnold." That is when I say, "Then ask them to validate their name and they will!!" Just ask your guide to show you a sign. Either you will see a personalized license plate that says Adam, or you will get a random phone call with someone asking if Arnold can talk. Your guides don't mess around!

One time I had a student put her guides to the test on almost a daily basis. She would say things like if you are with me I want to see two people jogging in purple pants today. And she WOULD! Haha, I don't know if our guides like to play "prove it" games, but I do know that they want you to know they are real, and they are helping you.

Oh, and did you know that you can send your guides out to help others? Yes, you sure can. Ever see a little girl crying because she fell off her bike or a lady who obviously is depressed? Send your guides for help, and they will send the little girl a butterfly and the depressed lady a random bouquet of flowers. How cool is that?

Strengthening communication with your guides: I am adding this inside this chapter but for the purpose of development, you may want to take a few days to meet your guide(s) before you continue onto this step.

Once you have met your spirit guides in some form, whether you see, hear, feel, or just know they are there, you will want to strengthen that communication. Some of you may have full on conversations with your guides and won't need this. For the majority of my students, the tools here have been helpful in having a better understanding of the information that is coming from your guides.

Note: Your guides will most likely not be using their lips to communicate with you. Some of my students would report back to me that their guide just stands there and doesn't say anything, and I always chuckle and remind them that they communicate with us via ESP or just a knowing.

All my guides and angels have taken up a placement around me. Some are to my right (main guides are usually to the right but not always), some are behind me, some are behind me and above me, and then there's Frank, who is directly in front of me facing me. Since I can see him, when I first started developing I gave him squares on the floor and a pointer stick. I would ask him to point to the squares showing me numbers for how old someone is or how many months or years until something would occur. Remember trusting and allowing what they say is crucial to your development. Frank and his pointer stick worked wonders for me to receive more information.

So play with the idea you can give your guides tools to help you receive information. Here are some other ideas that many of my students have found helpful to incorporate. Mind you, sometimes your guides are already ahead of the game and use these tools without you giving it to them.

Flashcards with initials or names

Movie screens with a scene being played out

Calendars with dates, months, seasons, etc.

Depending on your gift's strength at this time will be dependent on what tools you want to use. Like I said, some students, mostly "hearers"/clairaudience, will actually "hear" their guides and don't need any tools. I call them cheaters....haha, joking, sort of.

If you would like to listen to a guided meditation on how to meet your guides, I have one for you, because I'm cool like that. Just go to **brandaleen.com/resources.html**

Chapter 11: Angels

*Guardian Angel pure and bright guard
me while I sleep tonight.*

Are angels real? That's what I thought when I started developing my gift. In hindsight, I think I was crazy to think they weren't real. But because of my upbringing, I thought they were only for the Christian religions. Boy, was I wrong! Angels are the bomb!

Angels can be anywhere at any time to help you with anything! They are pure love, and they love you unconditionally. Yes, they want to help you find your keys, pay your bills, and even keep your thoughts in alignment with your goals. But the trick is, **you have to ask!**

We, humans, have free will to create our lives. That free will can't be interfered with, unless, from what I understand, we are to be saved from an untimely death, only then can the angles intervene. Otherwise, ask away! I ask for help with just about everything. I ask for help making my videos, writing this book, paying my bills, and I even ask for help eating healthy.

One question many people ask that I like to clear up right away is, if an angel is with you helping you find your keys, does that mean you are taking away from someone else that may need them for something more important? Absolutely not! When you understand there is no such thing as the concept of time or space, then you will know Angels can be anywhere at any time. They can be at the hospital helping with the surgery of a little girl at the same time they are at my house, or in your car, or by your bedside.

The great thing about angels is you don't need to know who to ask for, just ask and the angel that helps in that particular area will be there. If you choose to work with angels on a regular basis, you may want to learn a bit more. I have listed below the main archangels that I work with and what their specialty is.

Archangel Michael is probably the most known out of all the angels. He is the protector of all. You can call on him for protection over your energy, your house, your car, and even to protect you in situations and help you transition.

He is who you should call upon to "cut cords" from toxic people or situations. He can safely cut away any energetic attachments, leaving your energy clean and clear.

Michael is known to have the strongest presence and loudest voice. He is great to try automatic writing with because of this.

Colors: Royal Purple, Royal Blue, and Gold
Crystal or Gemstone: Sugilite

Archangel Raphael is the healing angel. His energy is green, and you can call him to assist you in any healing work. He can help heal your body, mind, and spirit. He also helps all healers in their work.

Color: Emerald Green
Crystal or Gemstone: Emerald or Malachite

Archangel Gabriel is the angel of communication. He is great to call on before any journaling, writing, or speaking work.

Gabriel is also helpful with children in regards to adoptions and birth.

Color: Copper
Crystal or Gemstone: Copper

Archangel Jophiel is known as the angel of beauty. She can help you keep your thoughts pure, assist you in finding the right outfit to adorn your body with, inspire you to bring beauty into your environment/home, and to help you see the beauty in all of life.

I call upon her every day and ask her to keep my thoughts in alignment with my path.

Color: Dark Pink
Crystal or Gemstone: Rubellite or Deep Pink Tourmaline

Archangel Metatron is commonly known as the angel of life. He oversees the Akashic Records and is directly connected to the Divine.

He facilitates incarnate humans experiencing the highest vibrations possible. He is a wonderful Archangel to call upon, therefore, for help with spiritual development and learning. He is also known as the Archangel who watches over indigo and crystal souls, and sensitive children in general, helping them channel their sensitivities for good and without fear.

Color: Violet and Green
Crystal or Gemstone: Watermelon Tourmaline

Archangel Ariel is the angel that works with animals, fish, birds, and our environment. She works closely with Archangel Raphael when doing healing work on these.

You can call on her to help you become more aware of what our environment needs and work with her in healing it.

Color: Pale Pink
Crystal or Gemstone: Rose Quartz

Archangel Uriel is great to call on for confidence in working with your intuition. He is also great to ask for answers in taking test or in a challenge. He can instantly "download" the information to you as an instant "knowing", also referred to as claircognizance.

Color: Yellow
Crystal or Gemstone: Amber

These are just a few of many, many more angels. These are the principal angels that I work with and just the tip of information on each one of them. Remember, they can't help unless you ask because of our free will. You don't need to memorize who does what, just ask for help and they will be there!

Angels can show up in so many different ways. You may see a flash of light out of the corner of your eye. You may see a huge pillar of light, and it may have different hues of color. You may see them in your mind's eye just as if they were in human form. You may have a feeling associated with them. For the longest time, I felt them like they were soft and fluffy like cotton candy or a cloud. It is difficult to describe that feeling, but that's the best I can do. Another example of how many people may see them is a sparkle, almost like a piece of glitter is floating. Angels can also appear as a humongous hue of light. Have you ever seen how the sky turns a different color before it storms? That is similar to what people who work with angels see over a church or an entire town. One of my great friends who works with angels said that she was attending church, and the priest was doing a talk on addictions. She described that all of the sudden it was like the entire church filled with a yellow hue, and she could see Archangel Jophiel. While Raphael is the healing angel, Jophiel helps with keeping our thoughts beautiful. I wanted to give you multiple examples of how people see angels because we all experience things differently and for you to discover the way that they are reaching out to you.

How to Connect with Your Angels

Sit quietly and be sure to be grounded and centered. Make sure to sit with your spine straight and your legs and arms uncrossed. Set your intention that you are now ready to meet your angel. You can imagine the room you are in filled with gold sparkles (angels love gold). Ask your personal guardian angel to come to you and then be open to receive any feelings, sensations in or on your body, emotions, etc. Angels work in a very subtle and soft way through your senses. Trust what you are feeling. Ask your angel what their name is and be open to what comes. What color is your angel? Ask them to step away and then step forward again as many times as needed until you can tell how it feels when they are near.

You will most likely feel the unconditional love that they have for you. It can be such an emotional experience that you may cry. I know I did! Knowing that someone or something loves you more than you even love yourself can be an emotional experience. We tend to feel unloved for some reason in our human experience. Make sure to journal about your experience each time.

Check out the resource section on my website for any guided meditations at brandaleen.com/resources.html

Working with Your Angels

Whether it is on your behalf or to help others, your angels want to work with you. Many of my students do very well with angel readings by calling on the angels and then delivering the messages they receive. Angels love to do healing work, counseling, comfort care, basically anything that has to do with helping people, animals, and mother earth. You just need to decide what your core reason for wanting to help people is and then ask them to work alongside you.

Angels love to leave you gifts, and signs

Angels will drop you a feather in the most random places as a gift or a sign. In my online development course, week 4 is what I call *Angel Week* In that week, I ask the angels to leave each one of my students a feather. Most always, by the end of the week, everyone has found at least one feather. The color actually has its very own message that comes along with the feather.

Black. Spiritual protection. Also, abundance is coming.

Black and white. Change is coming.

White. your angels are with you.

Pink. Love is in the air.

Blue. You have spiritual gifts. Your spiritual gifts are growing.

Gray. Peace is on the way.

Yellow. You are on the right track.

Spotted. Let go of what no longer serves you.

Other signs from your angels can be:

- Pennies or coins found in random places.
- Songs on the radio. They love to remind you they are thinking of you by putting on a song that resonates with your current situation. You will know when a song is a sign and not just a song.
- Butterflies or birds that catch your attention.
- Ringing ears. While this can also be tinnitus, when you are developing your intuition ringing in the ears can be a common occurrence. Because angels have an extremely high vibration, we may perceive their messages as a ringing in our ear.

- Repeating numbers! This one is a biggie. How many times do you see repeating numbers? 11:11 is what I like to call the awakening code. That is usually the number that people will start to see over and over when it is time for them to stop going through the motions and begin being present in their life and pay attention to more signs. There are some great websites that you can look up what numbers you keep seeing and find out the meaning.

- Angel clouds. When you just happen to look up, and there is a cloud shaped like an angel, it is not a coincidence. It is a sign that your angels are looking over you.

I truly love when the angels come forward in my readings. When they have something to say it is always, encouraging, loving, and gentle. No matter what darkness you feel you are going through, they are there and are nonjudgmental. They will love you no matter what you have gone through or how much you are judging yourself; they still love you and are with you!

Chapter 12: Ethics and Non-Judgement

"When you judge another, you do not define them, you define yourself."

- Wayne Dyer

It is important to use good practices when you develop your intuition and be respectful. If you are not, it is very likely that your spiritual team will remove your gifts.

As far as ethics, I teach my students to be very aware of the effect the messages we deliver has on others. For example, if you feel your client has an illness, and you say to them "you have XYZ illness" then that will forever be in their mind. They may come to manifest this dis-ease. While we do receive accurate information, when it comes to health I recommend that you tell them to seek medical attention. One thing I do mention to my clients is if I feel they need energy work to help align and clean their chakras, and energy, etc., but that is about the extent of my health readings.

The same concept should apply to reporting an upcoming death, problems in pregnancy, tragic accident, etc. Please be very aware of the impact you may make and be conscious of how you word your readings. If it were me, I would always focus on the positive and let them know to be careful while driving to work or always say I love you to loved ones because they can be gone in an instant.

There is an exception to this. If the client already knows they are ill and would like a medical intuitive reading, then you can deliver what you receive but still being mindful and make sure to cover yourself from any liability from the medical community by having and stating a disclaimer that you are not a medical professional, etc.

One thing I like to add here is to remember your boundaries and agreements with spirit because we only want information that is love and light only that will help our clients live their lives more fully. If you start getting too much negative health information, then revisit your boundaries and ask your spiritual team to shift what information they are sending you.

If the dark side, medical intuitive or death is your niche, and yes it is for some intuitives, then you need to sit with your team and find the best way to deliver the messages with love and light in mind to your clients.

Permission

You would think that asking permission before you tap into and read someone's energy would be a cut and dry subject, but it isn't. When I go to the grocery store, or anywhere for that matter, people tend to have information just floating on them for all to see. That type of information is unavoidable but continuing to tap into their energy after that point is like peeping into their bedroom window and not a healthy practice.

During readings, I will also be able to see (clairvoyance) into the lives of people who are around my client, such as husband, co-workers, etc. As far as I go with that is what their intentions are with my client. I do not go into detail about that person whom I see through the energy of my client without their permission.

Some living people may come through in a reading as a spirit. Yes, that sounds wild, but it happens. When this happens, and after you are developed enough to tell the difference between living & dead/spirit information coming in, you may deliver the information you receive about that person/spirit because you are essentially speaking to their soul and not imposing on their human ego.

Non-judgment

Non-judgement comes along with taming your ego through connecting with Source, pure consciousness, on a regular basis. Usually, meditation is the avenue for that and by the time you are delivering messages to clients non-judgment should already be in place. We are all on the same path of evolution but not necessarily at the same point on our path, so it is imperative that you are empathetic to that. Our creator wants nothing more than for all of us to be happy, and our creator also does not live in our society where there are rules to follow and boxes to fit in either. So, if someone comes to you and says they are cheating on their husband, it is your job to help them live their lives more fully, not condemn them with your egoic beliefs. Am I saying it is OK to cheat on your spouse? I'm saying it is none of our business as the medium and to deliver the loving guidance that spirit always offers. This may sound tough for some of you, but once you have absorbed the simple fact that we are one, then I believe that you will come to see pure love in all living creatures.

Chapter 13: How to Approach Games and Readings

"Intuition is a very powerful thing, more powerful than intellect."

- Steve Jobs

When we receive information from spirit, it is being filtered through our human experiences, our brain, emotions, memories, our five senses, etc. We each have a unique experience and so it is important not to allow our human brain to interfere with the information given to us. Spirit will show you, tell you, have you feel a certain way, so that you get the information. They don't want you to dissect the information. They just want you to "say the words." This is by far one of the most important challenges for a new intuitive because our human brains always want to figure out what it is that we are receiving and make it into something we can understand. A good friend of mine who trained along with me when we were developing our intuition said this, "You are to deliver the mail, don't open the envelope and read the letter, just deliver the mail." It is up to the client to figure out what the message means.

In my online courses I am a real stickler when I say that all I want for you to say is:

How do you feel?

What do you see in your mind's eye, your imagination?

Do you smell anything?

What do you hear?

What do you just seem to know?

Let me give you a few examples.

During the first week of my online development course, the students are asked to tell me what is behind a closed doorway. Without giving them the instructions above, they will start out by "guessing" what room it is. They will say it's a bathroom, a basement, a doctor's office, etc. However, when they just say how the door makes them feel, maybe they feel anxious or calm. What do they see in their mind's eye such as a large square shape, the color purple, soft, dark/light, open or crowded? What do they smell? Maybe they smell animals or incense. What do they hear? Maybe they can imagine hearing several voices behind the door, shuffling sounds, creaky wood, etc.

I promise if you stick to the basics and do not try to figure it out, you will find that you are on target by 99% more than if you allowed the human brain in to help.

If you are part of my private group community on Facebook, **Spiritual and Personal Development**, you will be able to see the comments of those trained by me and those that are just "guessing with their human brain" in the games that we play. If you are not a member, you will want to join so you can exercise your muscles on a regular basis. There is a link to join my group, among many other handy resources at **brandaleen.com/resources.html**

The technique I am sharing here with you should be used in every game or even a mediumship reading. Remember it is not your job to figure out why you are seeing, hearing, feeling or knowing something. It is your job just to say the words.

One of my students was asked to do a mediumship reading for me speaking to my grandmother. I love to give this as an example because it is perfect. Using the technique of being general, she said these things to me about my grandmother.

Socks (the kind you wear on your feet)

The color Red

Dogs

Beans

Chairs

This may sound EXTREMELY general. Some skeptics may roll their eyes at this, but the truth is these simple words mean the world to me and clearly validates that the student was speaking with my grandmother. The student probably thought she was dead wrong but let me share with you:

My granny always had fuzzy socks. During Christmas, the entire family would buy her more. It was our thing. Her favorite color was red, and she always wore it. She had several small dogs in her life, and the one who was alive at her passing disappeared two days following. We still can't figure it out. My granny made the best beans and cornbread, and she would always say that she needed to put on a pot of beans. And lastly, the chairs! Oh my gosh, she had the ugliest funky antique chairs that none of us liked. When she was getting bad with her Alzheimer's, she overheard us talking about getting rid of the chairs and her eyes got so big and she said she would roll over in her grave if we ever got rid of them. And you know what? My mom still has them.

I have another great example that I can share of leaving your human brain out of readings. A client was missing her glasses and reached out to me for help. I said this:

I see square glass windows. I see brown cement like flooring. I feel like I smell this funky smell. I am warm. I see some type of wool fabric with muted colors. The client was ecstatic at first and said you just described my entryway. She couldn't wait to get home to find her glasses. When she got home, she messaged me saying they weren't there. Two days later, she confirmed that she found them below the window in the basement, near the cement flooring, beside the dryer sheets, and there were muted colored blankets nearby. So I could have said, "I believe the glasses are in your entryway," and she would have never found them. Instead, I stuck to what did I see, hear, feel, know, smell, etc.

Keep it simple Sam and your gifts will soar to new heights!

CHAPTER 14: CLAIRVOYANCE

"Close both eyes to see with the other eye."

- Rumi

Clairvoyance is known as and psychic seeing or clear seeing. Some signs that your clairvoyant muscle is one of your stronger gifts (at this time) are:

- Do you find yourself daydreaming a lot?
- Did or do you have an imaginary friend?
- Do you experience déjà vu?
- Do you have vivid and in detail dreams?
- Have you ever dreamed something and it came true?
- Can you see ghosts?

Clairvoyance is your imagination, your third eye, your mind's eye. Let me share an example. Most everyone knows McDonalds and the golden arches. Close your eyes right now and can you see the golden arches in your head? That is your clairvoyance. Now, if you cannot see the McDonald's logo in your head, do not freak out, you are not broken. 30% of people don't see their imagination, and that is ok. Just think about blind people. Their other senses are heightened, and they get around and live life just like anyone else. If you can't visualize, you will find strength in your other gifts.

A developed clairvoyant receives information visually. It just so happens that my strongest gift is clairvoyance, so I will share some of the ways I receive information. As I shared in the earlier chapter on Agreements, my guides would show me colors in a flash. Once I put two and two together, through finding similarities in my readings, those colors were shown to me for particular reasons. For example:

White = medical energy, as in the person works in the medical arena. Nurse, Reiki practitioner, dental assistant, etc.

Pink = mother energy

Purple = grandmother in spirit who helps with spirituality

Yellow = death by suicide, or cancer

These colors are NOT universal and are my personal experience and agreements that are in place with my spiritual team. It all has to do with how you and your guides communicate.

A clairvoyant also can see visions of people, events, etc. from the past, present, and future without being there physically. This can be done while awake and also during dream time. It is literally as an image or vision is inserted into your head and as you learn to trust it enough to say what you see, more and more will come to you. In the beginning, I would have to close my eyes to "see" my clairvoyance but through exercise, I can see with all three of my eyes at the same time. Almost like an overlay of two television screens.

Developing clairvoyance exercises.

As with my online development courses, I recommend taking an entire week for each of the clairs (clairvoyance, clairsentience, clairaudience, etc.) and only focusing on the exercises for that particular chapter to get your muscles strong and then go onto the next or loop back around and start again. If you are like me, you will break the rules and read the entire book first. That that is OK, but remember this is a muscle. Just like you probably can't open the front door and run a marathon today, you will need to exercise it to develop it.

Meditate 15 minutes per day at least five days per week. This is hands down the most important exercise to developing your intuition and reestablishing your connection with source energy.

Journal about EVERYTHING, after meditation, waking, after guessing games, EVERYTHING.

Imagine what color someone will be wearing every day and get validation. Give yourself credit for what you get right. If you said they would wear a red dress, and you show up, and they have on a red belt, give yourself credit! See why you said what you said. Sometimes you may need to ask questions from the subject because you may find out they were wearing what you thought but then changed. Trust me; it happens more than you think. When I test my online students with this intuitive game, I give them credit for everything I've worn in the last 24 hours. Note: you are new to this and may pick up on the past, present, or future!

Visualize balloons of all different colors. Pick one at a time on which to focus. Focus on the red one, yellow, etc. Do this a few times a day.

Stare at the world around you. Really, really stare! This exercise is twofold. First, it brings you right here into the present moment, and secondly, it gets you to focus on minute things that you don't usually notice. So stare at the water running down the shower wall, stare at the paint on the wall, stare at the back of your hand, stare deeply into some form of nature, look how your feet touch the grass, etc. Do this for 15 minutes a day. Journal your findings.

Imagine what the parking spot you will get looks like. Take note of your findings.

Write down colors of the rainbow and what they mean to you. This will help you associate feelings with colors and may develop your agreements quicker.

Meditation – Visualize cleaning your third eye. I will sometimes literally imagine spraying my third eye with a cleaning solution and wiping it off. Where the attention goes energy flows!

Detox from heavy metals, fluoride, toxic chemicals from food and self-care products, etc.

Feed your third eye. Foods such as like purple grapes, blueberries, eggplant, purple cabbage, etc. are great to fuel your third eye. Wearing purple or indigo is excellent for your third eye as well as visualizing the indigo color swirling in a clockwise fashion at the point of your third eye.

Get a photograph of someone you don't know who will give you detailed feedback. Invite in their spirit guides, angels, and past loved ones, in love and light only, to help give you information. Also invite in your spirit guides, angels and past loved ones to assist you. Set an intention to receive information about this person. Sit down and have your journal handy. Write down any thoughts that come to you during that moment. Even if you think it is your thoughts at this moment, it is meant for you to write it down for your "client." Write down any sensations you get. It could be a feeling of anxiety, an ache in your right knee, visions of people, etc. Everything matters at this moment. When you finish it is important for you to share everything you wrote down with the subject, even if you are anxious that you made it up or are wrong. You have to trust and allow! Have the subject give you detailed feedback so you know what you got right, and you know why you said or felt certain things.

Remember to cut cords and ground down after doing any intuitive work because doing so brings your energy up to the top four chakras. You will want to bring it back down, or you will be left, open, vulnerable to energy, and feel spacey.

Do guided meditation to open your third eye.

Do visual based exercises and get validation such as the ones I use in my online development courses. See behind doors, remote viewing, and more.

Work with Archangel Raziel and ask to be surrounded with the highest vibrations of divine love and to heal or release any fears that are connected to my spiritual sight.

Make sure to check the resources for some free guided meditations at brandaleen.com/resources.html

Affirmations to opening your third eye.

- It is easy for me to visualize.
- I am willing to receive visual information.
- I easily develop a powerful and effective clairvoyant ability.
- I trust the visions that come to me.

Chapter 15: Clairaudience

*"Notice the loving guidance you hear
inside your mind and from other people."*

- Archangel Zadkiel

Did you spend a week on clairvoyance or did you cheat and skip ahead? Busted? It's OK, but make sure you do spend a week on developing each clair!! Let's go into clairaudience next.

Clairaudience is also known as psychic hearing, clear hearing. Often we experience clairaudience and confuse it with our own thoughts. Clairaudience is delivered in many forms. You can hear a voice outside your head. It can be a thought or a stream of thoughts that just seems to pop into your head from nowhere. It can be through external sounds like the TV, children screaming nearby, a song on the radio, a song in your head in the morning, high pitched ringing in your ears, and even actually hearing a real voice (male, female, tones, etc.) inside your head. This particular one has happened to me, and it can make you feel like you are going schizophrenic. Funny, not funny, right?

Trust me; I get all kinds of calls as a medium, and one of them is a concerned parent with a teenager that refuses to go to school because of all the voices in her head, or can't go to sleep because they won't leave her alone. This call happens more than you think.

Oh, you are probably asking, how can the TV or a random sound in my environment be clairaudience? When training my students, I tell them that no matter what happens during a reading or during an intuitive exercise that it is meant for the reading or exercise. For example, you sit down to call your client for a reading, and suddenly your kids go running past screaming like wild animals, or the TV suddenly gets loud and annoying. I would tell you to say something like, "Do you keep your TV on really loud or do you have a bunch of children in the house with you right now?" You will be surprised how often you get validation. Every single thing that happens at that moment is meant to say.

As with every aspect of your intuition, with clairaudience, it is important to trust what pops in your head or what you think about or hear enough to say the words to your client. The more you trust that very tiny voice, the louder it will become.

Clairaudience exercises:

Meditate 15 minutes a day!! This is going to be inside every single chapter I write about intuition development so start making it a practice to get your OM on every day. You can do this with the intent to just plug into Source energy or, for the purpose of this chapter, you can do some visualizations regarding your ear chakras opening {see below}.

Listen to the world around you. Really, really listen! First, sit quietly and be grounded and present. Then, listen to your breath, your heartbeat, your eyelashes and anything inside your body. Next imagine your ears are growing bigger and listen to the room where you are. Do you hear the clock ticking, electronics humming, etc.? Go bigger still and have your ears grow larger and listen to the entire building you are in and then immediately outside the building. Keep having your ears grow bigger and keep expanding. Imagine what your town sounds like, what the earth sounds like, what the cosmos sounds like. All the while your ears are growing bigger and bigger. When you are doing routine tasks this week such as washing the dishes or vacuuming, etc., listen to the sounds that accompany the tasks. Hear the dishes clinking, the hum of the vacuum, etc.

Listen to classical music for 20 mins a day and select a specific instrument and listen to it. Only focusing on that instrument for a few moments and then switch instruments.

Ask questions from your guides and ask them to give you the answers auditorily.

Imagine your ear chakras opening. Your ear chakras are governed by your throat chakras and are located on your cheeks by your lower jaw bone. You can take clear quartz and hold it there; you can visualize white light cleaning that area and also Lapis Lazuli is ideal for clairaudience.

Archangel Michael can help safely open up your clairaudient abilities. Ask him to vacuum away any lower energies in your ears or ear chakras. Be open to let go of anything painful you have ever heard in exchange for hearing the voice of love and the angels.

Get a photograph of someone you don't know that will give you detailed feedback. Invite in their spirit guides, angels and past loved ones, in love and light only, to help give you information. Also invite in your spirit guides, angels and past loved ones to assist you. Set an intention to receive information about this person. Sit down and have your journal handy. Write down any thoughts that come to you during that moment. Even if you think it is your thoughts, in this moment it is meant for you to write it down for your "client". Write down any sensations you get. It could be a feeling of anxiety, an ache in your right knee, visions of people, etc. Everything matters in this moment. When you are done it is important for you to share everything you wrote down with the subject, even if you are anxious that you made it up or are wrong. You have to trust and allow! Have the subject give you detailed feedback so you know what you got right and you know why you said or felt certain things.

Automatic Writing is an amazing tool for intuitive beginners, especially with clairaudience. See below for instructions.

Journal about your exercises, meditation, etc.

Automatic Writing:

This is a tool to receive information from your Spirit Guides, Angels, Passed Loved Ones, and even your own Inner Voice or Higher Self. Everyone can do automatic writing, and it is particularly useful to those that are new to developing their intuition.

Reasons why to do Automatic Writing

- If you need guidance in your life
- To receive information on behalf of another person
- To assist you in journaling, a blog post or writing a book
- When you are just learning to develop your intuition and don't know how to "hear" or "see" your guides yet

How to do Automatic Writing

The best time to do automatic writing is after a meditation. The meditation can clear your mind and get your conscious mind out of the way. Perhaps even meditate with the intention of why you are about to attempt automatic writing.

Have a pen and paper ready or a keyboard to type.

Set an intention as to why you wish to do this exercise.

Protect yourself by inviting in your spiritual team members in love and light only and surround yourself with the white light.

Ask for the energy that you wish to connect with (higher self, guides, etc.) to come forward. Ask for them to work with you, in love and light only, to give you the information as clean and clear as possible. I highly recommend asking for Archangel Michael as he is very loud and clear.

Now start to write down or type the question that you have.

Allow any thoughts or feelings you have and just write, write, write. It's important not to analyze, dissect or judge anything that comes through. You may notice that your hand is moving on its own without you having to think about it. Or you may have thoughts pop into your mind that you very quickly write. The key is to go with whatever happens without holding yourself back!

Once you feel the information has come through go, back and read what you wrote. Many times I will go back and be amazed at the quality and intelligence that came out and think, "Wow, now I KNOW I didn't write that." :)

Give gratitude and trust and allow!

Affirmations for developing clairaudience:

- I am powerfully clairaudient.
- It is safe for me to hear the voice of spirit.
- My hearing brings me joy and transformation.

- My ears are safely attuned to hear higher frequencies.

Chapter 16: Clairsentience

"The world is confusing; your spirit is not. The opinions of others are confusing; the wisdom of your inner voice is not."

- Sonia Choquette

Clairsentience is also known as psychic feeling or clear feeling. Clairsentience is the sense or intuitive muscle that allows you to receive information through your physical body through physical sensations as well as your emotions.

People who are clairsentient usually feel a physical sensation in or on their body which leads to information. For example, I am clairsentient and when information is coming in I can literally feel my stomach flip-flop. That is a sign for me to stop and pay attention. Then the sensations end up translating to information. For me, a flip-flop can translate to someone lives far way, someone is a dentist, an attorney, a father, needs to call his mother, etc. I know it sounds funny and other than describing it this way I can't quite explain how or why the feeling translates. Remember, everyone is different so, all clairsentients don't necessarily receive it the same way I do. Some of my clients and students feel a tingling sensation on their face which means a spirit is nearby and wants their attention, some of them get cold or hot feet, or some feel like they have bugs in their hair. We each receive it differently.

Another great example is goosebumps. I call those validation bumps because if I get goosebumps, it means a clear YES. It is a sign that I need to talk more about what I'm saying or go into greater detail that I am on target.

Abilities that clairsentients are good at would be:

- Knowing the happenings of a building or a piece of land without prior knowledge
- Feeling when someone steps inside a room
- The ability to touch objects and tell the history of it or to find missing objects and people, also known as psychometry
- Feeling the emotions of others around them which is not to be confused with empathy

Clairsentience Exercises:

Meditate 15 minutes per day!

Make a list of things to FEEL this week such as a dentist, a male, a female, California, Summer, sister/brother, Uncle, the ocean, etc. Sit down and make sure you are grounded and centered and have your journal handy. Allow yourself to explore how all of these different people, places, and things, really FEEL to you. What sensations does your body have? Do you feel a difference in your body with each of these? Do this several times this week.

Make a list of emotions to feel this week. Take a few minutes to feel each emotion and how it affects your body, and your chakras.

Ask a friend to send you a photo of someone you don't know and write down how you feel this person's life is. What is their personality like? Get validation!

Feel several objects this week. Note in your journal what do they FEEL like? What impressions do you get from various objects? Do they put off a vibration? Does it feel dead, as in no energy, or does it feel toxic, healthy, etc.?

Have someone hide an object that you are connected with from you and find it You won't want to go looking for where it would potentially be but rather BECOME the object and look around yourself. Essentially you are matching the vibration of the object and you look around yourself and see where you are. Is it dark, cold, open, crowded, are you on something soft or hard, etc.? You could also use a mapping technique by sensing if your body is getting warmer or colder just like when we were kids. This exercise can also be done with missing people so if you are good at it that may be your calling.

Take note of how all the various places you visit this week feel. Can you tell the history of the land or building? Can you tell what went on inside a certain establishment? Allow yourself to be open to the fact that you can tap into this information.

Do a few practice readings on people you know and see if you get sensations on or in your body when connecting with their energy.

Clairsentience comes into play when Spirit is around. If you feel comfortable invite in a passed loved one, in love and light only, who belongs to you and pay attention how your body feels. Do you feel pressure, short of breath, tingles, etc.? Journal your findings.

Affirmations to develop clairsentience:

- I am open to feel the energy of spirit.
- I am safe in developing my clairsentience.

Chapter 17: Claircognizance

"Claircognizance is the ability to know without trying."

- Lada Ray

Claircognizance also known as clear knowing. Someone with Claircognizance will know exactly what I am talking about when I say that you find yourself just knowing something. You have no idea why you know or how you came to know it, but you will almost fight to the death standing up for whatever it is because you clearly, without a doubt, know it to be true.

This aspect of my gift pops in on me now and then, and if you know me, you have probably heard me tell you my chicken story. My husband and I went to the store, and we only buy organic foods, especially any meats. The store we were at had two types of organic chicken. I don't know how I knew that one of them was NOT organic. I will probably never find out if I was right, but I still to this day just know it wasn't organic. My husband challenged me and asked, "How do you know?" I had to stand by my claircognizance and say, "I just do!"

Another example was a sudden knowing of how a wild weed in my yard would benefit my health. I don't know how I knew. Maybe the plant told me, but I knew.

As with empathy, claircognizance can and will develop alongside with your other intuitive muscles simply by developing and using them.

While there isn't really an exercise to develop claircognizance, one thing I suggest is to be present when you have a sudden knowing and journal about it or put it in the "save this for later file" in your mind. That way, when you do get validation, you will have something to go back on. Plus you will start to get a feel, if you will, for when this knowing is coming in and be able to utilize it better.

Since I didn't give you any exercises for this chapter, that means you get the green light to proceed on into empathy. Not that you are obeying the guidelines anyway, because, I rarely do.

Chapter 18: Empathy

"Empathy is about standing in someone else's shoes, feeling with his or her heart, seeing with his or her eyes. Not only is empathy hard to outsource and automate, but it makes a world a better place."

- Daniel H. Pink

Empaths are known to be extremely sensitive people that often have a hard time coping with the harsh environment in which we live. Let me start this chapter out with specific bullet points on what traits an empath has so you can narrow it down and see if this fits you.

An Empath:

Cares so deeply about others. This can mean society as a whole, their family, friends but especially the environment and animals. They often avoid watching the news because it is too harsh for them.

Is sensitive to others emotions without being told. An empath will try to fix things in their environment because that is better than them feeling the people around them being agitated, or emotional.

Is self-critical. An empath will often feel like it is their fault things aren't going right and will live in a place of self-judgement and self-abuse in some cases.

Is an introvert. This is because they'd rather stay home where it is safe versus feeling all the energy at the grocery store.

Takes on others emotions. Often empaths can go into the grocery store feeling happy but then leave a crying mess. That is because somewhere in the store that they either engaged with (store clerk) or where nearby someone who may have been very upset. The empath feels the emotions around them so deeply they will feel that this emotion must be their own. This happens because in our norm, we never talk about the possibility of being able to feel other people's emotions, and so they go on to act out as if that emotion is theirs. Often it can take hours for an empath to shake the feeling, especially if they don't realize they are an empath.

These are just a few examples of being an empath. There is a full questionnaire on my website that you can take at **brandaleen.com/resources.html**

As far as developing empathy, in my experience, most of the empaths that I have worked with often call it a curse and want to be protected from it. I believe that if you are an empath, you are an empath, no training necessary, but in developing your other invisible muscles (the clairs, etc.), you will use the empathy as a magnifier. An empath needs to ground, shield, and cut cords often! Sometimes multiple times per day. Grounding and shielding can help protect you against any harsh energy and cutting cords is imperative for an empath to disconnect from any energy to which they are connected. I have a beautiful guided meditation for this to share with you. Just pop over to the resource section on my website!

A perfect example of this is one of my clients could feel the cancer in her father-in-law and knew exactly where the tumors were in his lung. This is an energetic connection that should be cut. Another one of my clients worried so much about her sister's and mother's behavior towards her that she created massive cords to them. This connection drained her energy field so much so that her gift of sight, clairvoyance, was turned off by her guides to allow her to save her valuable life force energy. This particular client also has an autoimmune dis-ease, so it is crucial that any empath protects their energy.

When an empath combines empathy with their other intuitive muscles, they are known to be great with animal communication, health diagnosis (did I mention the majority of nurses are empaths?), emotional intuitives, not to mention they are fantastic at communicating with Angels!

Empaths and Angels:

In my experience, empaths are intimately connected to Angels because they are part Angel. This may sound crazy (I think I say that a lot), but that is what Spirit tells me. Angels are, well, hello, sweet as all get out, loving, pure, Godly, yeah all that! Ever notice how many empaths (not all) are somewhat overweight? That extra weight is a cushion for the harshness to bounce off. Kinda like an airbag in a collision.

One of my clients and dear friends, Stacie Danielle, is an empath, and she has gone on to develop an empowerment course specifically for her fellow empaths. I asked her to share with me for this book a bit about empathy and here is her contribution.

> "It is often said that being an empath is both a blessing and a curse. It is true that being an empath is an amazing, beautiful, powerful, and at

times, highly challenging gift. The power in the "soulular" connection- priceless and rare. Being an empath becomes a curse only if one is untrained in how to handle the gift or unwilling to acknowledge it and make holistic, mind-body-soul changes to live a balanced, gentle life. Life as an empath can be full, magical, and deeply loving!

The difference between being an empath and having empathy is that the empath actually feels others' feelings as if they were their own; whereas the person having empathy without being an empath experiences feelings more like care and compassion. The empath experiences both, along with actually being in the other person's "shoes," so to speak."

- Stacie Danielle

Oh, and one last thing for you empaths before you head on to the next chapter, I'm sending you big love! I can be about as brash as they come, but I try to slow down and send a little sugar to my empath friends. <3

Chapter 19: Mediumship

"Mediumship is a blending of consciousness, bridging the non-physical with the physical."

- Clair Broad

I have a lot to say about Mediumship. First, I will start with stating that we ALL have the ability to develop our mediumship. Just like your intuition, mediumship is a muscle. Mediumship uses all the intuitive muscles you have developed to receive the information. The difference with mediumship is you are receiving the information from an actual past loved one, a spirit who no longer inhabits a body, a meat suit, as I like to reference it. Mediums also receive their information from higher realms such as angels, guides, etc.

If it isn't mentioned in this book yet, then let me share that I am a self-developed medium. Meaning I had no prior experience or idea that I could communicate with loved ones on the other side until I went through a similar type of training as written in this book and offered in my online courses. Since then I have been teaching others to do the same, and it is amazing to witness a seemingly regular person develop the ability to deliver healing messages from past loved ones to their living friends and family.

Now, some people have their mediumship turned on and don't even know it. I call that your porch light. These people go about their daily lives and have no idea that a multitude of past loved ones and spirits, in general, are following them around or swarming them upon entering a public place. This, my friends, is where it gets juicy!

Mediums, who are walking around with their porch light on and don't know it, often experience the following:

- Anxiety
- Depression
- Afraid to be alone at night
- Diagnosed bipolar, with an autoimmune dis-ease, or even schizophrenic
- Thoughts pop into your head that don't seem to be you.
- Trouble with electronics

Find the full list and quiz on my website, **brandaleen.com**

I would like to address just a few of these individually.

Anxiety

When an undeveloped medium enters a public place with their porch light on, all the spirits can see it and feel drawn to it. They know that this undeveloped medium may have the ability to give messages to their living loved ones. When an untrained medium suddenly has several invisible people around them inside their personal space they start to feel "something" but they don't see anything and that can, and usually does, create an anxiety attack. Just think of it this way. If you have five living people come and stand right in your face, you would probably tell them to get out of your face and step outside your personal space. However, when those five people are spirits and invisible, that is when anxiety happens.

Depression

Same sort of scenario here. An undeveloped medium may feel the emotions of not only the living people around them but also the invisible dead people. If the invisible person standing near you died and didn't cross over or maybe were the cause of their death by suicide, they tend to "feel" sad and depressed. When you start to feel this emotion, you are obviously prone to think it is your own. I always tell my students to ask themselves, "Is this me? Do I have a reason to feel depressed right now?" This can also happen upon sleeping or waking because, remember, what I said, "They follow the light and may come home with you, ride in the car with you, etc.

Bipolar

People who are diagnosed bipolar often have mood swings. How I explain this into mediumship is being influenced by spirits, usually the not so nice ones. Remember the chapter on clairaudience, psychic hearing? Well, that comes into play right here. Sometimes the thoughts in our heads are psychic hearing. Psychic hearing comes from the invisible spirits. Spirits are just like living people. Some are fun and outgoing and positive, and some are Debbie Downers, low vibrational, etc. If a spirit can speak to you and also influence your emotions enough to act out, then it is an open invitation for them to continue to influence you how to behave. Here is an example of a scenario. You suddenly feel angry at your husband. You start expressing your feelings, and it escalates to you feeling enraged. You start saying things that you normally wouldn't and it keeps escalating. Suddenly you see yourself smacking him in the face and harming him, and you feel so angry you actually do it. Maybe he says to you, "What has gotten into you?" Think about it.

I have had a few students with a bipolar diagnosis, and one of them left me this review after taking my online development course. "I took Brandaleen's (then called) psychic boot camp 101. I learned much more from this class than I thought was possible. I took the class with the intention to learn to communicate with passed loved ones and came out of the class realizing that my bipolar diagnosis of 15+ years is wrong! I am a medium! Thank you so much Brandaleen for opening up my eyes and my soul so that I can live life to the fullest now!" (Jill Meyer reviewed Brandaleen Johnson — 5 star May 2, 2015)

Schizophrenia

This is a classic clairaudience scenario. Some, not all, mediums with clairaudient ability hear the "voices" and not a voiceless message, but the spirit's actual voice as it was when they were alive. This happened to me once while I was lying in bed when I went to visit my mother. I heard, in my head, other people's voices and what they were saying. Thank goodness I knew what this could be because I'm not going to lie, my first reaction was thinking I've gone crazy! And, any untrained medium probably would believe that they were going crazy. The thing that gets me thinking is how many mediums are on medication for something that can be fixed by developing your intuition and standing in your power. Up until now, any such symptom of hearing voices has always been addressed by the medical community. **Disclaimer. I am not a medical professional. I am by no means saying not to seek help should you hear voices, but rather sharing what I have learned through my experience. "Schizophrenia is characterized by abnormal social behavior. In severe cases, patients may see or hear things that aren't real." For a list of other symptoms, (www.nimh.nih.gov/health/topics/schizophrenia/index.shtml)

Autoimmune Diseases

When a medium is untrained or has their porch light on without their knowledge, spirits are attracted to that light. When a spirit steps into your energy field, it starts to drain it. If you are constantly having spirits around you trying to give you messages to deliver or simply following you around out of interest of your light, then your energy field can and will become drained without taking the necessary steps to disconnect from them and replenish your field. After years of this type of energy depletion, you may manifest dis-ease such as an autoimmune dis-ease because of your body's lack of immune system. When I meet a client with an auto-immune dis-ease, we work together on cutting cords, grounding down and creating boundaries from spirit as described in each of those topics in this book.

Different Types of Mediums

Throughout the many students I have had the honor of teaching, I have found that there are several different types of mediums, just like we all have our own personalities. There may be other names for the types of mediums I am about to describe, but these are how I have come to experience them.

Dreamers

Some mediums are what I call dreamers. The dreamers I have worked with either dream of an event that comes to pass, they have full conversations with their loved ones, they dream of themselves as another person going through a situation only to find that person later comes to them for a reading, etc. For example, one of my dreamers would dream every night about other people and the goings on of their lives, and eventually those same people (even strangers) would end up coming to her for a reading, and she would already know everything she needed to tell them. For dreamers, it is crucial to journal your dreams because the details need to be saved for a later date and time. Another reason why it is important for dreamers to journal is to let your spiritual team know what you did or did not see in the dream. If you journaled but didn't note down an important part of the dream, your team will then send it to you again. And if you do not journal your team will stop sending you information if they know you won't do anything with it in the first place.

Medical Mediums

Some mediums are amazing at doing health scans. I remember doing an exercise with some of my medical intuitives, and they did, what I believe, was just like having an MRI or a Pet/cat scan. Once the subject went to their medical doctor, the results were spot on with what the medium said. This is obviously a touchy subject due to medical laws, etc., so I tell my students always to recommend their client follow up with a medical professional

Paranormal Mediums

Some mediums are into all things creepy. They can see the creepers and have an inner knowing on how to help clients rid of them. They love doing paranormal work, visiting haunted places, crossing spirits over, and transmuting the dark back into the light. I do not enjoy working with the dark and think it is awesome to have these types of mediums for referrals.

Line them up!

While all mediums have the ability to speak to the dead, there are those who have an entire line of the dead outside their front door. The line is so long it can wrap around the world. These types of mediums are great with gallery readings when there is a large audience, and they can deliver messages from who steps forward in spirit.

Channels

Some mediums channel information from angels, light beings, alien races, etc. A good example of a well-known channel would be Esther Hicks who channels Abraham, a collective energy focusing on the law of attraction. Some mediums allow the dead to step inside them to deliver the messages through them by using their voice and body. I don't recommend that because of the energy drain, but there are those who have mastered that technique. I'll never forget the day it happened to me on accident. I had a lovely client come in for a reading. Her grandmother stepped forward in spirit and gave me some general information. It was all going like it normally does until the client asked me about her father's health. I looked (being clairvoyant), and I could see him walking slowly, breathing hard, and always lying on the couch. I was about to speak when I felt this sensation to my left and WHAM I said in a Marge Simpson type of voice, "And he sleeps on the couch." My client's grandmother had made her way inside my body and used my voice. I don't know who was more shocked my client or me. Her eyes were so big, and her mouth was wide open that my voice changed like that. I looked up to the sky and said, "That's not cool granny!" You can guess what my next boundary was, can't you?

Regardless of what type of medium you are, or become developed to be, remember you are the boss. Mediums should have several boundaries in place to let Spirit know when, where, and how they want to work with them. For example, I do not prefer to speak to the dead in public places like restaurants or the grocery store. It just isn't my thing and so on my list of boundaries I have that listed as a no-no. Do they still see me and talk to me? Yes, sometimes. But because they know my rules, they would be more likely to go towards someone else's porch light. Additionally, I have my hours of operation listed, and they are not allowed in my bedroom unless I invite them. Why have these boundaries? Because remember what I said about the energy drain and autoimmune dis-ease? Even if you are a developed medium, sometimes spirits can be around, and you may not notice them. They will drain your energy whether they are a nice spirit or not.

Developing Your Mediumship Muscle

This chapter is towards the end of this book for a reason. It is critical to have the right intentions and to have all your protection concepts understood and in place. You should fully understand grounding, cutting cords, boundaries, and you should have met your spiritual team (even if you can't see them) and have them be with you during any mediumship exercises. Your spiritual team should have your permission to send away any spirits that do not have a high vibration or who may have ill intentions. I work in love and light only and so should you. This is not a game, and the invisible realm is very real. When I prepare to speak to a past loved one I make a very clear statement: I invite my spirit guides, and angels in love and light only, and then I invite the spirit in love and light only, and they must be my vibration or higher. If the spirit's vibration is lower than mine, either I will not speak to them or will ask for one of their spiritual team members that is a vibrational match to translate.

For the purpose of developing this muscle first make sure you are grounded, set your intention as to why you are doing this exercise. Ask for your spiritual team to come in love and light only. Imagine yourself covered in a white light robe. You can also invite in the spirit's spiritual team with the intention that they will help give you the information.

Now ask for a spirit, preferably one you know and feel incredibly safe with, to come to you in love and light only to answer the following questions.

NOTE: Notice how you feel after you invite them in. Do you feel a difference in the air? Can you feel a presence? Do you see them? Many of my clients report different sensations on or even in their body when a spirit steps forward. Some feel like they have bugs in their hair, feel short of breath, feel tickles on their arm or leg, and even one of my students reported her feet turn cold when a spirit is around. Remember your boundaries: If you don't want to SEE dead people, put that on the list.

I always have my students ask a specific question because a spirit will show up and give you a bit of random information but then, just like a living person, will wait for you to ask. I have my students ask: How did you die? (Note: This is obviously for spirits that you don't already know the answer.)

Pay attention to your body here. Write down how it feels because that is a key on how they passed away. Also, what do you see, hear, feel, know, smell, and taste at this moment? Write it all down.

Ask, "What was your life like?" Write down anything that comes to you, even if you feel it is a memory of yours that counts at this moment.

When you complete the exercise cut cords (remember the white waterfall technique), ground down, and thank all the spiritual team members and the spirit for helping you.

The more important part is to get validation, validation, validation!!! That is the only way you will know if you are on point or to understand WHY you said certain things and be able to understand what you saw, heard, felt, smelled, knew at a later exercise. Keep an eye out for those agreements too! Agreements are imperative with mediumship.

As you develop this muscle, you will probably start having more visitors. For me, it started with dead people that belonged to me and then the dead that belonged to people that I knew. Because of my boundaries, I don't normally have random visitors, which I call roamers. However, many of my students do have random visitors, a stranger that came home following your light or maybe the neighbor's husband who passed, etc. NOTE: Do not speak to any spirit before you ask them if they are of the light. If they do not answer, say no, or avoid the questions, SEND THEM AWAY! It is just a good practice only to allow love and light spirits and only when you are prepared to work. Don't feel like you are rude.

These roamers often come as a prelude to a reading that will happen. Like the night before I do a psychic fair with multiple clients or before we do a Selfie Saturday event in my private Facebook Group, I will have a room full of loved ones who just can't wait for the event to start. I usually will acknowledge their presence and tell them to come back when it's time to work.

Chapter 20: In Closing

"Rule your mind or it will rule you."

- Buddha

Now that you have learned how to develop your intuition, I encourage you to keep exercising each intuitive muscle on a regular basis and they will grow and develop in a beautiful way. I recommend doing a practice reading at least once a week and do daily exercises using these intuitive muscles such as, what color will your husband wear, who is calling and why, etc. It is an excellent idea to sit down and decide what role you want to play in conjunction with your gifts. This human experience is yours, and you are the one who should decide how you want it to go. Let spirit know what it is that you want to do with them, and they will lead the way!

Remember this as well. Spirit will only bring you the people you can help. So if someone presents themselves to you and asks for a reading, don't freak out and let your ego tell you that you can't do it. Spirit brought this experience to you because, regardless of your skill level, only you, with your gift, your personality, your human experience, etc., can deliver the message that is needed. Spirit knows who can help who!

I sure hope that this book has given you a better understanding of your invisible muscles and the world in which they live, soul friends. <3

Lastly, I would love to have you join one of the online development courses I have in the near future. While the information in this book is included in the class, the online course offers much more, including the hands on experience. Trust me, we can all read books, but to apply what we learn, I feel that it truly comes down to the hands on exercises to get the most out of your development!

Love and light and trust and allow!

Made in the USA
Middletown, DE
10 June 2018